BIG BOOK OF STUPID JOKES

Other Smarties titles include:

Smarties Beautiful Beasties
Smarties Book of Wizardry
Smarties Chuckle Factory
Smarties Deadly Dinosaurs
Smarties Dinosaur Jokes
Smarties Guide to the Galaxy
Smarties Hairy Humans
Smarties Hilariously Funny Verse
Smarties How To Draw Cartoons
Smarties How To Make 'Em Laugh Joke Book
Smarties How To Be Really Smart
Smarties Joke Book
Smarties Knock Knock Jokes
Smarties Pirates
Smarties Practical Jokes
Smarties Puzzle Busters
Smarties Smart Art
Smarties Smart Science
Smarties Travel Teasers
Smarties Wacky World
Smarties Why the World Is Wonky
Smarties Wizard Joke Book

Smarties books are available from all good bookshops
or direct from the publishers on
+44 (0) 1206 255777

Smarties®

BIG BOOK OF STUPID JOKES

Compiled by Michael Powell

Illustrations by David Mostyn

Robinson Children's Books

ROBINSON

First published in Great Britain in 2003 by Robinson

This collection copyright © Constable & Robinson Ltd., 2003
Illustrations copyright © David Mostyn, 2003

NESTLÉ and SMARTIES are registered trademarks of Société des
Produits Nestlé S.A., 1800 Vevey, Switzerland.
© 2003 Société des Produits Nestlé S.A., Vevey, Switzerland.
Trade Mark Owners

15 17 19 20 18 16

A CIP catalogue record for this book
is available from the British Library.

ISBN 978-1-84119-712-8

Printed and bound in Great Britain by
CPI Group (UK) Ltd., Croydon, CR0 4YY

Papers used by Robinson are from well-managed forests
and other responsible sources

Robinson
An imprint of
Little, Brown Book Group
Carmelite House
50 Victoria Embankment
London EC4Y 0DZ

An Hachette UK Company
www.hachette.co.uk

www.littlebrown.co.uk

Contents

ADDLED
ANIMALS

Why can't a giraffe stand on its head?
Because it's too high up.

What did one pig say to the other?
'Let's be pen pals.'

How do you get an elephant into a telephone box?
Tell him it's a fridge.

When is an elephant most likely to enter your fridge?
When the door is open.

Why do elephants wear sandals?
To stop them sinking in the sand.

Why do ostriches bury their heads in the sand?
To look for elephants that aren't wearing sandals.

Did you hear about the stupid elephant?
He couldn't remember if he used to be forgetful.

How can you tell if an elephant is in your fridge?
The door won't shut.

Why do cows lie down when it's cold?
To keep each udder warm.

What do you get from a drunk chicken?
Scotch eggs.

Why can't you teach a frog to sing?
Because old ribbits die hard.

What animal never gets wet?
An umbrellephant.

What looks like an elephant, and can fly?
A flying elephant.

Why did the dinosaur walk on two legs?
To give the ants a chance.

What makes a chicken go red?
Henbarrassment.

Stuart: Did you know it take three sheep to make a jumper?
Jenny: I didn't know sheep could knit.

What did the cat say to the elephant?
'Meow.'

Why do the coyotes call at night?
The rates are cheaper.

Why do skunks smell so bad?
Because they wear cheap aftershave.

How many skunks does it take to stink out a room?
A phew.

Why do elephants stomp on people?
They like the squishy feeling between their toes.

Mary had a little cat,
Johnny had a pup,
Sarah had a crocodile that ate the others up.

What sound does a space turkey make?
'Hubble, Hubble, Hubble.'

What's even better than the cat's whiskers?
The bee's knees.

Why are giraffes brave?
Because they are always sticking their necks out.

How do you save a hippo drowning in hot chocolate?
Throw in a marshmallow.

What do sheep do on sunny days?
Have a baa-baa-cue.

Why didn't the female frog lay eggs?
Because her partner spawned her affections.

Where do elephants come from?
A great big stork brings them.

What does a stupid owl say?
'Twit-what?'

Why did the circus elephants get thrown out of the public swimming pool?
Because they kept dropping their trunks.

Why didn't the boy mouse like the girl mouse?
They just didn't click.

How can you tell if a bee is on the phone?
You get a buzzy signal.

Which is the better swimmer – a male ant or a
female ant?
Male, because it's buoy-ant.

Why did the ant-elope?
Nobody gnu.

What happened to the octopus who deserted from the army?
He had to face the firing squid.

If you had three octopuses in your wallet, how rich would you be?
You'd be squids in.

Where do polar bears vote?
At the North Pole.

Which fish go to heaven when they die?
Angel fish.

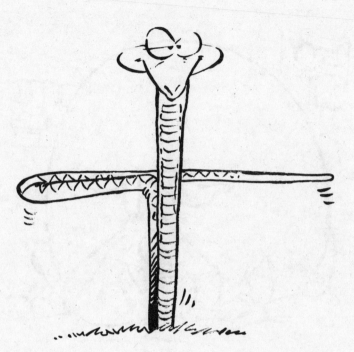

Rabbits can multiply, but only a snake can be an adder.

What did the mouse say after it broke its front teeth?
'Hard cheese.'

What happened when two American stoats got married?
They became the United Stoats of America.

What do bats sing when it's raining?
'Raindrops keep falling on my feet.'

Where do pigs go on their holidays?
Nowhere. They sty at home.

What did one amorous flea say to the other?
'I love you aw-flea.'

A chicken crossed the road and met James Bond.
'What's your name?' asked the chicken.
'Bond, James Bond. What's yours?'
'Ken, Chick Ken.'

Why did the stupid chicken climb over the glass wall?
To see what was on the other side.

Why don't bears wear socks?
Because they like to walk in their bear feet.

What did one firefly say to the other when his light
went out?
'Give me a push, my battery is dead.'

Why did the frog cross the road?
To see what was hoppining over there.

What does an elephant do if it breaks a toe?
Gives up ballet dancing.

First cow: Are you worried about Mad Cow Disease?
Second cow: Why should I be worried? I'm a helicopter!

How do you raise canaries?
Plant birdseed.

Why do giraffes have such long necks?
Because their heads are so far away from their bodies.

How did the octopus lovers walk along the road?
Arm in arm in arm in arm in arm in arm in arm in arm in arm.

If ants are such busy insects, how come they find the time to turn up at all the picnics?

How does a group of dolphins make a decision?
Flipper coin.

What is a toad's favourite ballet?
Swamp lake.

What is the last thing to go through a fly's mind
when it hits your windscreen?
Its backside.

Why do horses look sad?
Because they have long faces.

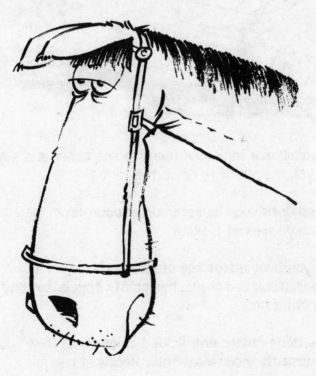

Two fish in a tank, one turns to the other and says,
'Do you know how to drive this thing?'

When does your hamster drive your car?
When you're not looking.

Did you hear about the stupid wolf?
It got stuck in a trap, chewed off three legs and
was still stuck.

Why don't rhinos eat pickled onions?
Because they can't get their heads in the jar.

Why do skunks argue?
Because they like to kick up a stink.

Penguin: What's your name?
Polar bear: My name is . . . . Stuart.
Penguin: Why the large pause?
Polar bear: I've always had them.

What's the worst thing about being an octopus?
Washing your hands before dinner.

What do snakes have on their bath towels?
'Hiss and hers.'

What do pigs use to write secret messages?
Invisible oink.

Why don't anteaters get sick?
Because they're full of anty-bodies.

Why are elephants so clever?
They have lots of grey matter.

What do rabbits put in their computers?
Hoppy discs.

What is a snake's favourite opera?
Wriggletto.

What musical key do cows sing in?
Beef flat.

Why did the gorilla log on to the Internet?
To send chimpanzee-mail.

How do you arrest a pig?
Put him in ham cuffs.

How do rodents keep their breath fresh?
They use mousewash.

What's black and white and eats like a horse?
A zebra.

How much did the psychiatrist charge the
elephant?
£100 for the consultation and £500 for a new
couch.

Which cat sailed round the world?
Christofurry Columbus.

Why do mother kangaroos hate rainy days?
Because the kids have to play inside.

Where do birds invest their money?
In the stork market.

What is smaller than an ant's dinner?
An ant's mouth.

What did the parrot say to the spaniel?
'I'm a cocker too.'

Which animal eats the least?
A polar bear, because it lives on ice.

Did you hear about the deer who took his driving test?
He did so well, the examiner passed the buck.

What should you do with a green elephant?
Wait until it gets ripe.

What's the definition of a caterpillar?
A worm with a fur coat.

How do really posh dogs send messages?
By pedigree-mail.

Why don't elephants smoke?
Because they can't fit their butts in the ashtray.

What would you do if you kept two hundred goldfish
in the bathtub and you wanted to take a bath?
Blindfold them.

Why did the cow jump over the moon?
Because the farmer's hands were cold.

How do you spot a bald eagle?
All its feathers are combed over to one side.

What does an octopus spend most of its money on?
Underarm deodorant.

What did the camel wear when he went into the
jungle to hunt?
Camelflage.

What did the boy sheep say to the girl sheep on Valentines Day?
'Wool you be mine?'

How do sheep sign their letters?
'Ewes sincerely.'

Name six things smaller than an ant's mouth.
Six of its teeth.

What is a chick after she's six days old?
Seven days old.

What does the bee Santa Claus say?
'Ho hum hum!'

Why do fish have such big phone bills?
Because once they get on the line they can't get off.

What did the dieting snake say when he was offered a piece of cheese for dinner?
'I'll just have a slither.'

Which insect can tell your fortune?
A gypsy moth.

What is out of bounds?
An exhausted kangaroo.

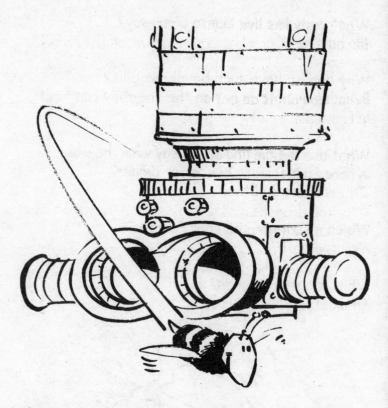

What buzzes, is black and yellow and sits at the bottom of the sea?
A bee in a submarine.

How do you stop a cow from mooing?
Use a moofler.

What kind of bears like to go out in the rain?
Drizzly bears.

How do you milk a mouse?
You can't – the bucket won't fit under it.

Why do sharks live in salt water?
Because if they were in pepper water they would sneeze.

What do robins do before exercise?
Worm-ups.

What is a caterpillar afraid of?
A dogerpillar.

Why are dragons most happy during Ramadam?
They enjoy eating knights.

How do you get milk from a polar bear?
Rob its fridge and run like mad.

What monkey can fly?
A hot air baboon.

Why do elephant tusks stick out?
They can't afford braces.

What do sheep say at Christmas?
'Season's Bleatings!'

Why did the elephant sit on the marshmallow?
So he wouldn't fall into the hot chocolate.

There were two cows in a field. One says 'Moo' and the other one says 'Hey, I was about to say that.'

Why does a milking stool have three legs?
Because the cow has the udder.

What happens if you put a glow-worm in water?
It becomes a floodlight.

Why do elephants wear green tennis shoes?
So the grass stains won't show.

Why do polar bears have fur coats?
Because the seals laughed at them when they wore parkas.

What did the traffic warden say to the frog who was illegally parked?
'Hop it, or you'll get toad away.'

What's green and dangerous?
A frog stampede.

Why are anteaters good workers?
Because a little aardvark never hurt anyone.

What goes 'snap, crackle and pop'?
A firefly with a short circuit.

Why did the elephant put his trunk across the road?
To trip up the ants.

Why shouldn't you tell a pig a secret?
Because pigs are squealers.

What's brown and pink?
A llama stinking his tongue out.

Why did the crab get arrested?
Because he was always pinching things.

Why are eggs going up?
Because the hens are lying on their backs with their legs in the air.

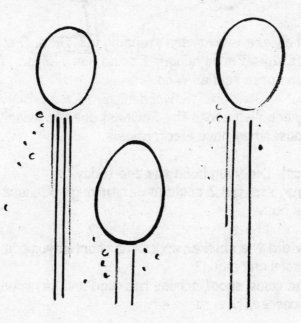

There were two horses standing in a field. One horse says 'I'm so hungry I could eat a horse.' The other horse replies 'Moo'.

Why are fish boots the warmest ones to wear? Because they have electric 'eels.

Stuart: Did you phone the zoo today?
Jenny: Yes, but I couldn't get through because the lion's busy.

Why did the chicken cross the road with a pair of scissors and a gun?
So he could shoot across the road and cut round all the corners.

What is black and yellow and buzzes along at
30,000 feet?
A bee in an aeroplane.

What would happen if tarantulas were as big as
horses?
If one bit you, you could ride it to hospital.

Where do birds meet for coffee?
In a nest-café.

Why don't elephants ride bikes?
They don't have a thumb to ring the bell.

What is a sheep's favourite sport?
Baaaaadminton.

Where do penguins build their igloos?
In coldisacs.

What do angry mice send to each other at
Christmas?
Cross mouse cards.

What did one worm say to the other when he was
late home?
'Where on earth have you been?'

What was the chicken doing in the woods?
Having a peck-nic.

What's a baby turkey called?
A goblet.

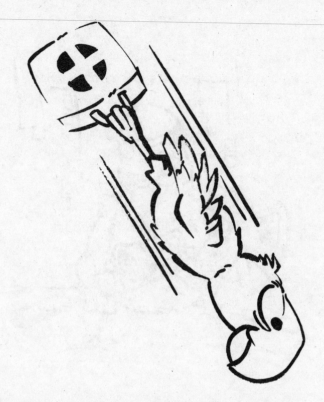

Who do you call when your parrot falls off his perch?
The Parrot-Medics.

What bird can write underwater?
A ballpoint penguin.

How do sheep keep warm?
Central bleating.

What do porcupines have that other animals don't?
Baby porcupines.

What is a canary's favourite computer game?
Tweet Fighter.

How can you tell if a skunk is broken?
When it's out of odour.

What do cows produce when it's hot?
Evaporated milk.

Why did the chicken walk on the telephone wire?
She wanted to lay it on the line.

What's the slowest horse in the world?
A clotheshorse.

Why can't penguins keep secrets in the South Pole?
Because their teeth keep chattering.

What fish does a builder use?
A pneumatic krill.

What do you call a bear with no ear?
B.

Who lost a herd of elephants?
Big Bo Peep.

Why did the pig run away from the pig sty?
He felt the other pigs were taking him for grunted.

What is an insect's best chat-up line?
'Excuse me, but is this stool taken?'

How do you know that chickens do overtime?
Because they work around the cluck.

How does a bird with a broken wing land safely?
It uses its sparrowchute.

How do chickens dance?
Chick to chick.

Why did the lizard go on a diet?
It weighed too much for its scales.

What do polite sheep say?
'After ewe.'

How do you get five hundred Pikachus in a tube train?
You Poke-em-on.

Why did the cow-pat cross the road?
Because it was a stand-in.

What noise annoys an oyster?
A noisy noise annoys an oyster.

Which insect is always dropping things?
A fumble bee.

What eats its victims two by two?
Noah's shark.

What does a caterpillar do on New Year's Day?
Turns over a new leaf.

Why did the parrot wear a raincoat?
So it could be polyunsaturated.

Why don't owls mate when it's raining?
Because it's too wet to woo.

How does a frog become invisible?
It uses a croaking device.

What do you call a rich rabbit?
A millionhare.

Why do elephants never forget?
Because nobody ever tells them anything.

What did the beaver say to the tree?
'It's been good gnawing you.'

What animal wears a coat when it's cold and pants
when it's hot?
A dog.

Why do pigs never recover from illness?
Because you have to kill them before you cure them.

How do nits travel abroad?
On British Hairways.

How can you lift an elephant?
Plant an acorn under it and wait twenty years.

What's green and slimy and goes 'hith'?
A snake with a lisp.

What do sardines call a submarine?
A can of people.

How do you save a drowning rodent?
Use mouse to mouse resuscitation.

Did you hear about the idiot who made his chickens
drink boiling water?
He thought they would lay hard boiled eggs.

Who is a wasp's favourite singer?
Sting.

Which hand would you use to grab a poisonous snake?
Someone else's.

Why did the ram crash his car?
He didn't see the ewe turn.

Baby skunk: Mum, why can't I have a chemistry set for my birthday?
Mother skunk: Because it would stink the house out.

Did you hear about the duck who had a nervous breakdown?
He quacked up.

What animal goes 'clip clip'?
A horse hopping.

What sort of maths do cows do?
Cowculus.

What's a porcupine's favourite food?
Prickled onions.

What clothes do fleas wear to work?
Jump suits.

What kind of creature is made out of wood?
A timber wolf.

Where do mice put their boats?
At the hickory dickory dock.

Why is Turtle Wax so expensive?
Because turtles have such tiny ears.

What do yaks gossip about?
The latest gnus.

Where does a down-and-out octopus live?
On squid row.

Where do ants go for their holidays?
Frants.

Why did the pig go to the amusement arcade?
To play the slop machine.

What's a kangaroo's favourite computer game?
Mortal Wombat.

What's grey and wrinkly and jumps every twenty seconds?
An elephant with hiccups.

What do you do if you find a tiger in your toilet?
Wait until he's finished.

What do pigs drive?
Pig-up trucks.

What goes 'ooo, oooo, oooo'?
A cow with no lips.

How do mice celebrate when they move house?
With a mouse warming party.

How do you catch a unique rabbit?
You neek up on it.

How do you catch a tame rabbit?
Tame way you caught the other one.

Why did the snake want to become a priest?
He got the coiling.

What do pigs take when they are sick?
Pigicillin.

What do you call a cow wearing a crown?
A dairy queen.

Why didn't the worms enter the ark in an apple?
Because they had to go in pairs.

What's a fish's favourite song?
Salmon-chanted evening.

What's red on the outside and white and grey on the inside?
An elephant hiding inside an envelope in a post box.

Why do bees buzz?
Because they can't whistle.

Why did the duck get kicked out of his flat?
He put too many quacks in the wall.

What goes thump, thump, thump, squish?
An elephant with one wet shoe.

How do you know that albatrosses are smarter than chickens?
Have you ever heard of Kentucky-fried albatross?

With which song did the bull woo the cow?
'When I fall in love it will be for heifer.'

How could the squid afford to buy a house?
He prawned everything.

What did the banana say to the monkey?
Nothing. Bananas can't talk.

Which racquet sport do elephants play?
Squash.

What should you write on a chicken's gravestone?
'Roast in Peace.'

What kind of tie does a pig wear?
Pig's tie.

Why didn't the anteater?
Because it was aardvark.

Where do milkshakes come from?
Nervous cows.

What goes 'peck, bang, peck, bang, peck, bang'?
A bunch of chickens in a mine field.

What did the baby chick say when he saw his
mother sitting on an orange?
'Look what marma-laid!'

Which fish can perform operations?
A sturgeon.

What's more dangerous than being with a fool?
Fooling with a bee.

Name a famous insect painter.
Pablo Beecasso.

What's a bear's favourite pasta?
Tagliateddy.

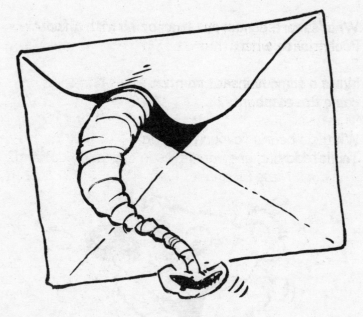

What's white on the outside and grey on the inside?
An elephant hiding inside an envelope.

Where do bees go on holiday?
Stingapore.

Why did the bee start talking poetry?
He was waxing lyrical.

Why was the centipede late for school?
Because he was playing 'This Little Piggy' with his
baby brother.

What has fifty legs but can't walk?
Half a centipede.

What is worse than an alligator with toothache?
A centipede with athlete's foot.

What's grey, has a wand, huge wings and gives
money to elephants?
The tusk fairy.

What's big and grey and lives in a lake in Scotland?
The Loch Ness Elephant.

Why are elephants grey?
So you can tell them from flamingos.

What's the difference between an elephant and a banana?
Have you ever tried to peel an elephant?

Why do elephants eat raw food?
Because they don't know how to cook.

How do you know that peanuts are fattening?
Have you ever seen a skinny elephant?

Two mice ran up the clock. The clock struck one and the other one got away with a minor injury.

Why do elephants have trunks?
Because they would look silly carrying suitcases.

Why are four-legged animals bad dancers?
Because they have two left feet.

What do you call a three-legged donkey with one eye?
A winky wonkey.

What goes 'dot dash, dot dash, neigh'?
Horse code.

What did the comedian say to the cattle rancher?
'Herd any good ones lately?'

What did the horse say when he got to the end of his nose-bag?
'This is the last straw!'

What's sweet but has sharp teeth?
A chocodile.

What's the only jungle animal that can scare a shark?
A chompanzee.

What does a triceratops get from scrubbing floors?
Dino sores.

BATTY
BOOKS

Why did the librarian slip and fall on the library floor?
Because she was in the non-friction section.

NEWSFLASH: Two lorries carrying ten thousand copies of Roget's Thesaurus crashed this afternoon. Witnesses were stunned, startled, aghast, taken aback, stupefied . . .

Stuart: Do you like Kipling?
Jenny: I don't know, I've never kippled.

What's a witch's favourite book?
Broom at the Top.

What is the Abominable Snowman's favourite book?
War and Frozen Peas.

Joe: Can I borrow that book of yours, How To
Become A Millionaire?
Sandra: Sure.
Joe: Thanks, but half the pages are missing.
Sandra: What's the matter? Isn't half a million
enough for you?

What did the astronaut say to the author?
'I took your book into orbit and I couldn't put it
down.'

When the Cold Wind Blows by I. C. Blast

Electric Shocks by Lou Swyres

Taming Lions by Claude Bottom

The Road To Damascus by Esau D. Light

Telling Jokes by Paula D. Otherone

Toilet Trouble by Enid A. Wee

The Closed Door by Russ T. Lock

Is This Seat Taken? by M. T. Space

How To Keep Warm by N. A. Huddle

How To Be Bossy by Colin D. Shots

How I Won the Grand National by Rhoda Winner

Inside the Church by Rosa Pews

Nobody Like Me by Percy Cueshun

My New Glasses Are Rubbish by Seymour B. Fore

Bubbles in the Bath by Ivor Windy Bottom

Talk Quietly by Dawn Shout

The Bank Robbery by E. Mustapha Dun-It

How to be Stupid by M. T. Head

How to Bake Biscuits by Gary Baldi

A Hole in the Rug by Fred Bare

Computers Made Simple by Mike Rochips

What do you call a building with lots of storeys?
A library.

What do young ghosts write their homework in?
Exorcise books.

Where do librarians keep their bees?
In the archives.

What Goes Well With Eggs by Chris P. Bacon

My Life as a Porter by Kerry Mibags

Who wrote Great Eggspectations?
Charles Chickens.

My father gave me a really cheap dictionary for my birthday.
I couldn't find the words to thank him.

What's a chicken's favourite book?
Cluckleberry Finn.

What kind of fish can you see in a library?
A microfiche.

Mike: Have you read *Harry Potter and the Order of the Phoenix*?
Allison: Yes.
Mike: What's it about?
Allison: It's about seven hundred pages.

All of my schoolbooks have pictures in them even if
I have to draw them myself.

Mum: Why don't you ever bring any books home?
Son: Because they're schoolbooks, not home books.

What's worse than carrying a lot of schoolbooks
home?
Having to open them once you get there.

What has a spine but no bones?
A book.

The history teacher caught Suzy drawing in her
textbook. She said, 'What do you think you're
doing?'
Suzy replied, 'I'm making my mark in history.'

The Bitter Blow by Major Setback

Forty Days in the Wilderness by I. Malone

Gone With The Wind by Rufus Blownoff

Vegetable Gardening by Rosa Cabbages

My Silver Wedding by Annie Versary

The Pearl Diver by Xavier Breath

Life in the Army by Marsha Lott

Did you hear about the dachshund's autobiography?
It's a long story.

Did you hear about the bloodhound's autobiography?
It got on the best smeller list.

Around the Mountain by Sheila B. Cumming

Silence in Court by Laura Norda

Missing You Already by Miles Apart

Showjumping by Jim Karna

I Can't Play Football by Mr Goal

Improve Your Garden by Anita Lawn

I Hate School by Gladys Friday

How To Be Annoying by Percy Cute

The Runaway Horse by Gay Topen

Feeling Worried by Anne Guish

Don't Jump Off The Roof, Dad by Luke B. Foryouleap

The Arrival by Neil E. Here

Fade Away by Peter Owt

CRAZY
CROSSINGS

What do you get when you cross a broomstick with a motorcycle?
A broom, broom, broom stick.

What do you get if you cross a snake with a pig?
A boar constrictor.

What do you get if you cross a serpent with a trumpet?
A snake in the brass.

What do you get if you cross baked beans with onions?
Tear gas.

What do you get if you cross a spider with an elephant?
I don't know, but if you see one crawling across the ceiling, run before it collapses.

What do you get if you cross a hyena with some gravy?
A laughing stock.

What do you get if you cross a donkey with Christmas?
Muletide greetings.

What do you get if you cross a biscuit with a suit?
A smart cookie.

What do you get if you cross bread with a bell?
Bunting.

What do you get if you cross a ton of prunes with the collected works of Shakespeare?
A loose canon.

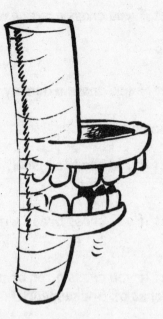

What do you get if you cross teeth with candy?
Dental floss.

What do you get if you cross a cow with a car?
A cattlac.

What do you get if you cross a camel with a duck
and a small bird?
A hump-quack quail.

What do you get if you cross an elephant with a
bird?
A gulp. It's like a swallow, only bigger.

What do you get if you cross a banana with a clown?
Peels of laughter.

What do you get if you cross a donkey with a jacket potato?
A donkey jacket.

What do you get if you cross a tuna with a lifeguard?
A fish that whistles to keep itself out of deep water.

What do you get if you cross a flat fish with a canary?
A cheepskate.

What do you get if you cross a cow with a werewolf?
A burger that bites back.

What do you get if you cross a bag of snakes with a cupboard of food?
Snakes and Larders.

What do you get if you cross a zombie with a boy scout?
A creature that scares old ladies across the road.

What do you get if you cross an anteater with a dog?
An aardbark.

What do you get if you cross a dog with a hippopotamus?
A mud hound.

What do you get if you cross a werewolf with someone who makes ceramics?
A hairy potter.

What do you get if you cross a tractor with a dog?
A Land Rover.

What do you get if you cross a rabbit with an aeroplane?
The hare force.

What do you get if you cross a skeleton with a feather and a joke book?
Rib ticklers.

What do you get if you cross a rabbit with a giraffe?
An animal that can eat very tall carrots.

What do you get if you cross a skunk with a bee?
Something that stinks and stings.

What do you get if you cross some nuns with a chicken?
A pecking order.

What do you get if you cross an artist with a police officer?
A brush with the law.

What do you get if you cross a musician with a
turtle?
Slow Rock.

What do you get if you cross a Cocker Spaniel with
a poodle and a rooster?
A Cockapoodledoo.

What do you get if you cross a parrot with a
woodpecker?
A bird that talks in Morse code.

What do you get if you cross a giraffe with a dog?
An animal that barks at low flying aircraft.

What do you get if you cross honey with a chair?
Sticky buns.

What do you get if you cross a hairdresser with a
werewolf?
A creature with an all over perm.

What do you get if you cross a plumber with a field
of cow-pats?
The poohed piper.

What do you get if you cross a skunk with an
octopus?
An octopong.

What do you get if you cross a four leaf clover with poison ivy?
A rash of good luck.

What do you get if you cross a Christmas tree with an apple?
A pineapple.

What do you get if you cross a computer with a flying carpet?
A mouse mat.

What do you get if you cross a pelican with a zebra?
Across the road safely.

What do you get if you cross a chicken with a centipede?
Enough drumsticks to feed an army.

What do you get if you cross a tomcat with a
Pekinese?
A Peeking Tom.

What do you get if you cross a worm with a spider?
A webcrawler.

What do you get if you cross a dog with a chicken?
Pooched eggs.

What do you get if you cross a PC with an elephant?
A computer with a really big memory.

What do you get if you cross a rabbit with a
shellfish?
The Oyster Bunny.

What do you get if you cross a bell with a bee?
A real humdinger.

What do you get if you cross a terrier with a vegetable?
A Jack Brussel.

What do you get if you cross a snake with pasta?
Spaghetti that wraps itself around your fork.

What do you get if you cross a cow with a carpet?
A thick pile all over the floor.

What do you get if you cross a lake with a leaky
boat?
About halfway.

What do you get if you cross a laptop computer
with a rhino?
A squashed lap.

What do you get if you cross a gymnast with a
book?
A book that can turn its own pages.

What do you get if you cross a bear with a freezer?
A teddy brrrrr.

What do you get if you cross a telephone with a pig?
A lot of crackling on the line.

What do you get if you cross a hovercraft with a polar bear?
A cross-channel furry.

What do you get if you cross a hedgehog with a giraffe?
A long-necked toothbrush.

What do you get if you cross a choir boy with a plate of mince?
A hymn-burger.

What do you get if you cross a vampire with a plumber?
A drain in the neck.

What do you get if you cross a dog with a skunk?
Rid of the dog.

What do you get if you cross a jogger with an apple pie?
Puff pastry.

What do you get if you cross a dog with a frog?
A dog that can lick you from the other side of the road.

What do you get if you cross a pair of trousers with a telephone?
Bell-bottoms.

What do you get if you cross a hyena with a Rottweiller?
I don't know, but if it laughs you'd better join in.

What do you get if you cross a small fly with an angler?
A fishing gnat.

What do you get if you cross a worm with a cake?
Fluky pastry.

What do you get if you cross a Labrador with a tortoise?
A dog that will run to the shop and bring back last week's newspaper.

What do you get if you cross a wireless with a hairdresser?
Radio waves.

What do you get if you cross a pig with a box of itching powder?
Pork scratchings.

What do you get if you cross a porcupine with a snake?
Barbed wire.

What do you get if you cross a chicken with some cement?
A bricklayer.

What do you get if you cross a hula dancer with a boxer?
A Hawaiian punch.

What do you get if you cross a dog with a cheetah?
A dog that chases cars and catches them.

What do you get if you cross a tin opener with a vampire and a cricket team?
An opening bat.

What do you get if you cross a turkey with some cement?
Gobblestones.

What do you get if you cross a farmer with an astronaut?
A ploughman's launch.

What do you get if you cross a footballer with a mythical creature?
A centaur forward.

What do you get if you cross an Italian landmark with a ghost?
The screaming tower of Pisa.

What do you get if you cross a book with a pound of fat?
Lard of the Rings.

What do you get if you cross a leopard with a bunch of flowers?
A beauty spot.

What do you get if you cross a sports reporter with
a vegetable?
A common tater.

What do you get if you cross a monster with a
chicken?
Free strange eggs.

What do you get if you cross a maths teacher with
a golfer?
A teetotaller.

What do you get if you cross a skunk with a pair of
rubber boots?
Smelly wellies.

What do you get if you cross a bed bug with a shy person?
A nervous tick.

What do you get if you cross a bottle of washing-up liquid with a mouse?
Bubble and squeak.

What do you get if you cross a telephone with an iron?
A smooth operator.

What do you get if you cross a Mexican snack with a tortoise?
Turtilla chips.

What do you get if you cross a pair of dogs with a hairdresser?
A shampoodle and setter.

What do you get if you cross a vampire with a mosquito?
A very itchy neck.

What do you get if you cross Charlotte Church with some washing-up liquid?
A soap opera.

What do you get if you cross an idiot with a watch?
A cuckoo clock.

What do you get if you cross a telephone with a fat football player?
A wide receiver.

What do you get if you cross a mountain with a baby?
A cry for Alp.

What do you get if you cross a sweater with a small fish?
A roll-neck herring.

What do you get if you cross a cow with a crystal ball?
A message from the udder side.

What do you get if you cross a crocodile with a camera?
A snapshot.

What do you get if you cross a maths teacher with a piece of furniture?
A multiplication table.

What do you get if you cross a tiger with a cabbage?
Man-eating coleslaw.

What do you get if you cross a glow-worm with a python?
A twenty-foot-long strip light that can squeeze you to death.

What do you get if you cross an ape with a cow-pat?
Monkey business.

What do you get if you cross an elephant with a whale?
A submarine with a built in snorkel.

What do you get if you cross a fish with bad breath?
Halibut-osis.

What do you get if you cross a large computer with a beefburger?
A big mac.

What do you get if you cross a scythe with a kitten?
A lawn-mewer.

What do you get if you cross a pig with a naked person?
Streaky bacon.

What do you get if you cross a blue cat with a red parrot?
A purple carrot.

What do you get if you cross an elephant with a bottle of whisky?
Trunk and disorderly.

What do you get if you cross a chicken with a cow?
Roost beef.

What do you get if you cross a compass with a shellfish?
A guided mussel.

What do you get if you cross a computer virus with a vampire?
A nasty byte.

What do you get if you cross a vampire with a boomerang?
A pain in the neck you can't get rid of.

What do you get if you cross a T-rex with a dog?
Something that drinks out of any toilet it wants to.

What do you get if you cross a toad with a newsreader?
A croaksperson.

What do you get if you cross an inventor with a vampire?
Something new fangled.

What do you get if you cross a dog with a maze?
A labyrinth.

What do you get if you cross a cat with a gorilla?
An animal that puts you out at night.

What do you get if you cross a skin doctor with an elephant?
A pachydermatologist.

What do you get if you cross an elk with a penguin?
Chocolate moose.

DAFT
DIFFERENCES

What's the difference between a dog with fleas and a bored guest?
One's going to itch and the other's itching to go.

What's the difference between a dog with rabies and a hot dog?
One bites the hand that feeds it, the other feeds the hand that bites it.

What's the difference between a kangaroo and a matterwitchoo?
What's a matterwitchoo?
Nothing. I feel fine, thanks.

What's the difference between climate and weather?
Climate is what you expect, weather is what you get.

What's the difference between a teacher and a battery?
A battery has a positive side.

What's the difference between a fish and a bicycle?
They can both swim, except for the bicycle.

What's the difference between the bagpipes and a trampoline?
You take off your shoes when you jump on a trampoline.

What's the difference between a spider and an Internet hacker?
One uses a web to trap bugs off a log, the other uses a web to log in and bug people.

What's the difference between a boring teacher
and a boring book?
You can shut the book up.

What's the difference between a smart Alec and a
man's question?
One is a wise guy and the other is a guy's why.

What's the difference between a football and a
duck?
You'll find one in a huddle and the other in a puddle.

What's the difference between a burger and a
bogey?
A burger goes on the table, a bogey goes under it.

What's the difference between a duck with one wing and a duck with two wings?
Well, that's a difference of a pinion.

What's the difference between head lice and nits?
A real nit is too stupid to find your head.

What's the difference between a cobra having a good time and a tanning salon?
One is snake fun and the other is fake sun.

What's the difference between a hunter and a fisherman?
A hunter lies in wait and a fisherman waits and lies.

What's the difference between a well dressed man and a dog?
The man wears a suit, the dog just pants.

What's the difference between a bus driver and a cold?
A bus driver knows the stops and a cold stops the nose.

What's the difference between a cat and a comma?
One has claws at the end of its paws, the other is a pause at the end of a clause.

What's the difference between a very old, shaggy Yeti and a dead bee?
One's a seedy beast and the other's a deceased bee.

What's the difference between a boxer and a man with a cold?
One knows his blows and the other blows his nose.

What's the difference between a nail and a bad boxer?
One is knocked in and the other is knocked out.

What's the difference between a dog and a painter?
One sheds his coat and the other coats his shed.

What's the difference between a mongrel and a pedigree dog?
About three hundred pounds.

What's the difference between a hungry person and a greedy person?
One longs to eat and the other eats too long.

What's the difference between a soldier and a young lady?
One faces the powder, the other powders her face.

What's the difference between see and sea?
You can see the sea but the sea can't see you.

What's the difference between a flea and a wolf?
One prowls on the hairy and the other howls on the prairie.

What's the difference between an elephant and a gooseberry?
A gooseberry is green.

What's the difference between Prince Charles and a javelin.
One is heir to the throne, the other is thrown in the air.

What's the difference between someone who needs the toilet and someone who is very ill?
One is dying to go, the other is going to die.

What's the difference between a rabbit and a giraffe?
A rabbit doesn't look like a giraffe.

What's the difference between electricity and lightning?
You don't have to pay for lightning.

What's the difference between a person with toothache and a rainstorm?
One roars with pain, the other pours with rain.

What's the difference between a weasel and a stoat?
One is weasely recognised and the other is stoatly different.

What's the difference between an iceberg and a clothes brush?
One crushes boats and the other brushes coats.

What's the difference between a duck?
One of its legs is both the same.

What's the difference between a robber and a
church bell?
One steals from the people, the other peals from
the steeple.

What's the difference between a buffalo and a
bison?
You can't wash your face in a buffalo.

What's the difference between ammonia and
pneumonia?
One comes in bottles, the other comes in chests.

What's the difference between a jogging rabbit and
a cross-eyed rabbit?
One's a fit bunny and the other's a bit funny.

What's the difference between a hill and a pill?
A hill is difficult to get up and a pill is difficult to get down.

What's the difference between a sigh, a car and a monkey?
A sigh is oh dear, a car is too dear and a monkey is you dear.

What's the difference between a photocopier and the flu?
One makes facsimiles, the other makes sick families.

What's the difference between a girl and a postage stamp?
One's a female, the other's a mail fee.

What's the difference between frustration and panic?
Frustration is the first time you discover you can't do it the second time.
Panic is the second time you discover you can't do it the first time.

DIZZY
DOCTORS

Doctor, doctor, every time I look in the mirror I feel sick. What's wrong with me?
I don't know but your eyesight is perfect.

Doctor, doctor, you have to help me out!
Certainly, which way did you come in?

Doctor, doctor, I've just been bitten on the leg by a dog.
Did you put anything on it?
No, he seemed to like it as it was.

Doctor, doctor, I can't stop my hands shaking.
Do you drink a lot?
Not really. I spill most of it!

Doctor, doctor, how long have I got to live?
Well, put it this way: would you like me to boil you
an egg before you go?

Why did the light bulb visit the doctor?
It kept having hot flashes.

Doctor, doctor, I keep thinking I'm an elephant.
Well sit on the floor then. I don't want you to break
my couch.

Doctor, doctor, I burnt myself making pancakes.
Oh, how waffle!

Doctor, doctor, do you make house calls?
Yes.
Then call my house and tell my wife I'll be late for dinner!

Doctor, doctor, what's that pain in my stomach?
You have acute appendicitis.
I came here to be treated, not flattered!

Doctor, doctor, I keep seeing pink spots.
Have you seen an optician yet?
No, just pink spots.

Doctor, doctor, I'd like to leave my body to medical science.
Don't bother. We couldn't find a cure for it.

Did you hear about the dentist who became a brain surgeon?
His drill slipped.

Doctor, doctor, people tell me I'm a wheelbarrow.
Don't let them push you around.

What did the surgeon say when he finished the operation?
'That's enough out of you.'

Psychologist: How many ears does a cat have?
Patient: Two.
Psychologist: How many eyes does a cat have?
Patient: Two.
Psychologist: How many legs does a cat have?
Patient: Haven't you ever seen a cat?

Doctor, doctor, I can't stand being three feet tall any longer.
Then you'll just have to learn to be a little patient.

Doctor: That's quite a cough you have there, what are you taking for it?
Patient: I don't know. What will you give me?

Doctor, doctor, I feel like an apple.
We really must get to the core of this.

Doctor, doctor, how can I make my cough better?
Practise, practise, practise.

Doctor, doctor, I think I'm invisible.
I can't see you today.

Doctor, doctor, have you got something for a bad headache?
Of course. Hit yourself in the head with this hammer, then you'll have a bad headache.

What did the foot doctor say to the movie star?
'There's no business like toe business.'

Doctor, doctor, my wife thinks she's a lift.
Tell her to come in.
I can't. She doesn't stop at this floor.

Outraged patient: The doctor can't see me for a month? I could be dead by then!
Doctor's receptionist: If so, can you ask your wife to cancel the appointment?

What did one tonsil say to the other?
'You'd better get ready, the doctor is taking us out.'

Doctor, doctor, how do I stop my nose from running?
Stick out your foot and trip it up.

Doctor: You need new glasses.
Patient: How did you guess?
Doctor: I could tell the moment you walked in through the window.

Why did the doctor put his wife under the bed?
He thought she was a little potty.

Doctor, doctor, can I have a second opinion?
Of course, come back tomorrow!

Doctor, doctor, my wife thinks I'm mad because I like peas.
There's nothing wrong with that. I like peas, too.
Great! Come back to my house and I'll show you my collection.

Doctor, doctor, I think I'm Napoleon.
How long have you felt like this?
Ever since Waterloo.

Doctor, doctor, I think I'm a frog.
What's wrong with that?
I'm about to croak.

Doctor, doctor, I keep talking to myself.
What's wrong with that?
I'm a salesman and I keep selling myself things I
don't want.

Doctor, doctor, I think I'm a biscuit.
You do look a little crummy.

Doctor, doctor, everyone thinks I'm a liar.
I can't believe that!

Doctor, doctor, I keep thinking there are two of me.
Well, don't both talk at once.

Doctor, doctor I keep thinking I is mad.
I am mad.
You as well?

Doctor, doctor, I think I'm turning into a fence.
Well, don't let that come between us.

When did medicine first appear in the Bible?
When God gave Moses the tablets.

Doctor, doctor, I can't get to sleep.
Sit on the edge of the bed and you'll soon drop off.

Doctor, doctor, a grasshopper just swore at me.
Don't worry. It's just a nasty bug that's going around.

Doctor, doctor, I keep thinking I'm a doctor.
Stop talking to yourself.

Doctor, doctor, my hair keeps falling out. Can you give me something to keep it in?
Yes, a paper bag.

Doctor, doctor, I feel as sick as a parrot.
Sorry I can't help you, you'll have to see a vet.

Doctor, doctor, I want to paint myself all over in gold.
Yes, you have a gilt complex.

Doctor, doctor, I keep thinking I'm a flea.
I thought you looked a little jumpy.

Doctor, doctor, I keep thinking I'm a horse.
How long have you felt like this?
Ever since I won the Grand National.

First dad: What is your son doing these days?
Second dad: He's at medical school.
First dad: What's he studying?
Second dad: Nothing, they're studying him.

Doctor, doctor, I think I'm a crocodile.
Well, there's no need to snap at me.

Doctor, doctor, I'm at death's door.
Don't worry. I'll pull you through it.

Doctor, doctor, I think I'm a shoe.
Well, stick out your tongue then.

Doctor, doctor, my wife thinks she's a chicken.
How long has she been this way?
About three years. I would have come sooner, but
we needed the eggs.

Doctor: Have your eyes ever been checked?
Patient: No, they've always been brown.

Doctor, doctor, I keep dreaming of aardvarks, bats,
hedgehogs, porcupines, yaks and zebras.
How interesting. Do you always dream in
alphabetical order?

Doctor: Now tell me how you burned both your ears.
Patient: I was doing the ironing when the telephone
rang, and I picked up the iron and put that to my
ear by mistake.
Doctor: But you burned both your ears.
Patient: That's because as soon as I put the phone
down it rang again.

Doctor, doctor, I think I've been bitten by a vampire.
Drink this glass of water.
Will it make me better?
No, but I want to see if your neck is leaking.

Doctor: How does your head feel today?
Patient: As good as new.
Doctor: It should be as good as new – it's never been used.

Doctor, doctor, I can't stop telling lies.
You're right. There's absolutely nothing wrong with you.

Doctor, doctor, my daughter has swallowed a bullet.
Well don't point her at me.

Did you hear about the plastic surgeon who went
sunbathing?
He melted.

Doctor, doctor, I can't stop pulling ugly faces.
What's the problem?
The people with ugly faces don't like it.

Doctor, doctor, I can't seem to make any friends,
you fat slob . . .

Doctor, doctor, I just swallowed a dog.
How does your throat feel?
Ruff!

Doctor, doctor, my husband smells like fish.
Poor sole!

Doctor, doctor, I've got a little sty.
Then you'd better buy a little pig.

Doctor, doctor, I keep thinking I'm a canary.
I can't tweet you. Go and see a vet.

Doctor, doctor, I've only got an hour left to live.
Can you come back tomorrow?

Doctor, doctor, I keep thinking I'm a magnifying glass.
You're blowing things out of proportion.

Doctor, doctor, I keep thinking I'm a moth.
So why did you come to see me?
I saw a light in your window.

Doctor, doctor, I snore so loudly I keep myself awake.
Sleep in another room then.

Doctor, doctor, I think I'm a dog.
Take a seat.
But I'm not allowed on the furniture.

Doctor, doctor, I keep dreaming there are monsters playing chess under my bed. What shall I do?
Hide the chess set.

Doctor, doctor, I think I'm turning into a pig.
How long have you felt like this?
A weeeeek!

Doctor, doctor, I'm so ugly. What can I do?
Hire yourself out for Halloween parties.

Doctor: There's no change in you since your last appointment.
Patient: That's funny, because I've just swallowed fifty pence.

Doctor, doctor, I can hardly breathe, I can't walk, I keep having palpitations and I'm covered in sores. Can you help me?
No, but I can recommend a good undertaker.

Doctor: You seem to be in excellent health, Miss Smith. Your pulse is as steady and regular as clockwork.
Miss Smith: That's because you've got your hand on my watch.

Doctor, doctor, I'm on a diet and it's making me irrational. Yesterday I bit someone's ear off.
Mmm, that's a lot of calories.

Doctor, doctor, I keep pulling ugly faces.
Don't worry, nobody will notice any difference.

FLIPPED OUT FOOD

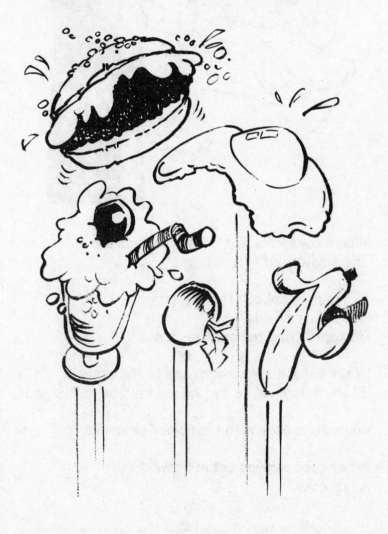

Which cake lives in a French cathedral?
The flapjack of Notre Dame.

Did you hear about the wizard who turned his
friend into an egg?
He kept trying to poach his ideas.

What did one strawberry say to the other?
'If you'd listened to me, we wouldn't be in this jam.'

Rhubarb: celery with high blood pressure.

What cake can you eat in heaven?
Angel cake.

Why are eggs overrated?
Because they're not all they're cracked up to be.

Why are sausages rude?
Because when you cook them they spit.

What kind of nut hangs on the wall?
A walnut.

Which herb can't keep a secret.
Thyme.
Why?
Because thyme will tell.

Did you hear about the lazy grape stomper?
He got fired for sitting down on the job.

What do swimmers eat off?
A pool table.

Why are hamburgers better than hot dogs?
Because hot dogs are wurst.

Are hamburgers male?
Yes, because they're boygers, not girlgers.

Which vegetables are found in the toilet?
Leeks and peas.

Why don't melons run away to get married?
Because they cantaloupe.

What did the widowed mother turkey say to her
disobedient children?
'If your father could see you now, he'd turn over in
his gravy.'

'Dad, what's for dinner?'
'Enthusiasm Stew. I've put everything I've got into
it.'

What does a skeleton order at a restaurant?
Spare ribs.

Farmer's wife: Do you like baked apples?
Farmer: Yes, why?
Farmer's wife: The orchard's on fire.

Which vegetable goes best with jacket potatoes?
Button mushrooms.

Why did the teacher have her hair in a bun?
Because she had her nose in a hamburger.

How long should you cook spaghetti?
About thirty centimetres.

What's brown and sneaks around the kitchen?
Mince spies.

What vitamin tastes salty?
Vitamin C.

Can a hamburger marry a hot dog?
Only if they have a very frank relationship.

How do you know when your chicken is cooked?
Check your roast watch.

How do you make an orange laugh?
Tickle its navel.

What is hairy and coughs?
A coconut with a cold.

What disasters could happen if you dropped a roast turkey?
The downfall of Turkey, the break-up of China and the overthrow of Greece.

What is a skeleton's favourite vegetable?
Marrow.

'Stop reaching across the table like that. Haven't you got a tongue?'
'Yes, but my arm's longer.'

Why can't the customers get into the fish and chip shop?
Because the fish fillet.

Why couldn't the sesame seed leave the casino?
Because he was on a roll.

Why shouldn't you eat on an empty stomach?
You should eat on a plate.

What did one snowman say to the other snowman?
'Can you smell carrots?'

How do you know if you have enough honey?
Conduct a beesibility study.

'What's a bear's favourite cakes?
Chocolate-y claws.

I trained my dog not to beg at the table.'
'How did you do that?'
'I let him taste my cooking.'

How do you start a pudding race?
Say go.

What happened when the Swede died?
There was a huge turnip at his funeral.

What's a shark's favourite pudding?
Leg custard.

What's a fresh vegetable?
One that insults a farmer.

Mother moth to baby moth: If you don't eat all your cotton, you won't get any satin.

Why did the pickle stay home from school?
Because he felt dill.

Where do turkeys go when they die?
To oven.

What do health inspectors have for breakfast?
Roached egg on toast.

Is it OK to eat food with your fingers?
No. You should eat your fingers separately.

'They're not going to grow bananas any longer.'
'Why not?'
'Because they're long enough already.'

What food can defend itself?
Kung-Food.

Louisa: I've been banned from cookery lessons because I burnt something.
Mum: Well that doesn't sound too bad. What did you burn?
Louisa: The school down.

Why is a banana skin on a pavement like music?
Because if you don't C sharp you'll B flat.

Did you hear about the stupid cook who tried to write a cookbook?
It came out of the typewriter burnt.

What is served in glasses and is hard to swallow?
A stiff drink.

Did you hear about the farmer who ploughed his field with a steamroller?
He wanted to grow mashed potatoes.

What is Beethoven's favourite fruit?
Ba-na-na-na, Ba-na-na-na.

Why did the sandwich go to the dentist?
Because he had lost his fillings.

How did the jury find the hamburger?
Grill-ty as charred.

What pie can fly?
A magpie.

What kind of nuts sneeze the most?
Cashews.

Where does a burger sleep?
On a bed of lettuce.

Why did the baker stop making doughnuts?
He got sick of the hole business.

Why didn't the banana snore?
It was afraid to wake up the rest of the bunch.

How do you make a green omelette?
Use one yellow egg and one blue one.

When is it all right to drink milk from a saucer?
When you're a cat.

Why is it impossible to starve in the desert?
Because of all the sandwiches there.

Why do idiots hate chicken soup?
They can't get it to stay on the fork.

How do you make a meat loaf?
Send it on holiday.

What did the grape say to the raisin at Christmas?
'Tis the season to be jelly.'

What's a vampire's favourite fruit?
Nectarine.

What is yellow and brown and hairy?
Cheese on toast dropped on the carpet.

Tom: Mum, can I have the wishbone?
Mum: Not until you've finished your greens.
Tom: But I want to wish I won't have to finish them.

Tom: Can I have two pieces of cake, please?
Mum: Sure. Take this piece and cut it in two.

Where do hamburgers box?
At an onion ring.

What are the most musical parts of a turkey?
The drumsticks.

Why do lions eat raw meat?
Because they don't know how to cook.

How do you fix a broken pizza?
With tomato paste.

What song do burgers sing on the job?
Gristle While You Work.

What kind of food do you eat in a taxi?
Corn on the cab.

What did one plate say to the other?
'Lunch is on me.'

What is the most unreliable vegetable?
A fickle onion.

What is a pizza's favourite relative?
Aunt chovy.

Why are cooks cruel to animals?
Because they batter fish.

Where does seaweed look for a job?
In the 'Kelp-wanted' adds.

What grace should you say before eating a salad?
'Lettuce pray.'

What is the opposite of a somersault?
A winter pepper.

Which soldiers smell of salt and pepper?
Seasoned troopers.

Why didn't the hot dog star in the movies?
The rolls weren't good enough.

Can an orange box?
No, but a baked bean can.

What did the hot dog say when he won the race?
'I'm the wiener.'

Why did the orange go to the doctor?
He wasn't peeling very well.

What's the best way to raise strawberries?
With a spoon.

Which vegetable has the sweetest rhythm?
Sugar beet.

How can an Irish potato change its nationality?
By becoming a French fry.

Juliet: Whisper something sweet in my ear.
Romeo: Double chocolate chip ice cream.

What do you call it when a cake goes clubbing?
Abundance.

What's a burger's favourite dance?
The char char char.

Why did the banana go out with a prune?
Because he couldn't find a date.

When can you count on a fish in an emergency?
When the chips are down.

First man: I've just been stung by a bee.
Second man: How was that?
First man: I was charged £50 for a pot of honey.

What's the difference between an American banana
and an English banana?
About 3,000 miles.

What is brown and hairy with yellow skin?
A coconut disguised as a banana.

Did you hear about the taxi driver who found a pair
of kippers in the back of his cab?
The police told him that if no one claimed them
within six months, he could keep them.

Which is the left side of a pizza?
The side that isn't eaten.

Why do the French eat snails?
They don't like fast food.

Graham: I've heard that eating fish is good for the brain.
Cathy: Me too, I eat it every day.
Graham: Oh, so it is an old wives' tale after all.

Paul was caught by his mother in the pantry.
'What do you think you're up to?' she asked angrily.
'I'm up to my eleventh mince pie.'

What's brown and hairy and wears sunglasses?
A coconut on holiday.

What do you call a revolving orange?
A merry-go-rind.

FOOLISH
FAMILIES

Sophie: My dad drives like lightning.
Sarah: He drives fast?
Sophie: No, he hits trees.

Did you hear about the child who was so ugly that his parents hired an actor to play him in their home movies?

Jamie: My dad's learning to be a pilot. Tomorrow his instructor says he can fly solo.
Jack: How low?
Jamie: He didn't say.

Tom: Dad, do you believe in free speech?
Dad: Of course, son.
Tom: Good. Can I use the phone?

Mum: Don't eat with your knife.
Jamie: But my fork leaks.

Sarah: Dad's just been arrested.
Mum: What's the charge?
Sarah: Nothing. They arrested him for free.

Did you hear about the stupid family that got
frostbite at a drive-in cinema?
They went to see 'Closed for the Winter'.

Dad: I'll teach you to throw stones at the
greenhouse.
Tom: It's OK Dad, I know how to do it already.

My dad took his car to be fixed, and told the mechanic: 'Check everything but the horn – it's the only thing that doesn't make a noise.'

Louisa: Dad, can I use your car?
Dad: What are your feet for?
Louisa: Left foot clutch and right foot accelerator and brake.

Mum: I got an anonymous letter today.
Dad: Really? Who was it from?

My sister talks so much that when she goes on holiday, she has to spread suntan lotion on her tongue.

Bro: What's the weather like out there?
Sis: I don't know, it's too foggy to tell.

Jamie: Mum, I bought you some toilet water for your birthday. It cost £20.
Mum: You shouldn't have. I can get it from the toilet any time I want, for free.

'My granny's teeth are like the stars.'
'White and sparkling?'
'No, they come out at night.'

Sis: Can I share your sledge?
Bro: Sure. We'll go half and half. I'll have it on the way down and you can have it on the way up.

Mum: Are your feet dirty?
Sophie: Yes, but I've got my shoes on.

Sis: Do you like warts?
Bro: No.
Sis: Don't worry. They'll grow on you.

Allison: I like your jumper.
Claire: Thanks. It's a hunting jumper.
Allison: Why is it called that?
Claire: Because my sister will have to go hunting for it.

Johnny: When I grow up I want to drive a train.
Dad: Well, I won't stand in your way.

Little Brother: If you broke your arm in two places, what would you do?
Big Brother: I wouldn't go back to those two places, that's for sure.

Did you hear about the outlaws' party?
One outlaw's wife's mother turned up because she thought it was an in-laws party.

Sophie: How old are your grandparents?
Sarah: I don't know, but we've had them ever such a long time.

Louisa: Mum, why do I keep going round in circles?
Mum: Shut up, or I'll nail your other foot to the floor.

Tom: Dad, can I have another glass of water, please?
Dad: But that's the tenth one I've given you tonight.
Tom: Yes, but my bedroom is still on fire.

Sis: Who gave you that black eye?
Bro: No one gave it to me. I had to fight for it.

Jamie: My mum eats like a bird.
Sophie: You mean she hardly eats a thing?
Jamie: No, she eats slugs and worms.

How do you know if your little brother is turning into a fridge?
See if a little light comes on whenever he opens his mouth.

Jimmy: Mum, are the Smiths very poor people?
Mum: I don't think so, Jimmy. Why do you ask?
Jimmy: Because they made such a fuss when their baby swallowed a coin

My dad's a light eater. As soon as it's light, he starts eating.

'Does your brother keep himself clean?'
'Oh, yes, he takes a bath every month whether he needs one or not.'

Mum: What are you doing Sophie?
Sophie: Writing my brother a letter.
Mum: That's a lovely idea, dear, but why are you writing so slowly?
Sophie: Because he can't read very fast.

Dad: Why is your sister crying?
Tom: Because I told her she was stupid.
Dad: That's not very nice. Tell her you're sorry.
Tom: Sis, I'm sorry you're stupid.

Holly: Mum, why is your hair going grey?
Mum: Probably because you wear me out with all
your questions.
Holly: You must have asked Granny lots then.

Mum: If you eat any more cake you'll burst.
Louisa: OK, Mum – just pass the cake and run for
cover.

'Hello, please will you put your sister on the phone
so I can speak with her?'
'But she's only a baby.'
'That's OK, I'll wait.'

My sister is so keen on road safety that she always wears white at night. Although last winter she was knocked down by a snow plough.

My sister was two-thirds married once. She turned up, the minister turned up, but the groom didn't.

I'm not saying my sister is annoying but she could give a headache to an aspirin.

Dad: Who broke the window?
Sarah: It was Jamie, Dad. He ducked when I threw a stone at him.

Jamie: My sister's the school swot.
Tom: Does she do well in exams?
Jamie: No, but she kills a lot of flies.

Dad: Why did you put a toad in your sister's bed?
Jamie: I couldn't find a spider.

What do a vulture, a pelican and parents have in common?
Big bills.

Sophie: Girls are smarter than boys, you know.
Oliver : I didn't know that.
Sophie: See what I mean.

My sister has lovely long red hair all down her back.
Pity it's not on her head.

Mum: What's happened to you?
Tom: I fell in a puddle.
Mum: But you've soaked your best trousers.
Tom: I'm sorry, Mum, but I didn't have time to change them on the way down.

If a whale mum had a son and daughter, what relation would they be?
Blubber and sister.

Mum: What did I say I'd do if you disobeyed me?
Sophie: My memory must be as bad as yours, I can't remember.

'My uncle's got a wooden leg.'
'That's nothing, my auntie has a wooden chest.'

Mum: Be careful, Jamie, most home accidents happen in the kitchen.
Jamie: I know, Mum. I have to eat them.

Tom: Mum, you've got a face like a million dollars.
Mum: Have I really?
Tom: Yes, it's green and wrinkly.

I reckon Mum must be at least thirty years old. I counted the rings under her eyes.

Uncle Simon: What's your new baby's name?
Ellie: I don't know. He can't talk.

Sarah: Mum, do you file your nails?
Mum: No. When I cut them off, I throw them away.

Tom: Mum, do you want me to leave home?
Mum: No, why do you say that?
Tom: Because you always wrap my lunch in a road map.

Little Sister: When I grow up I'm going to marry the boy next door.
Big Sister: Why?
Little Sister: Because I'm not allowed to cross the road.

Stuart: My parents don't like me at all.
Jenny: Why?
Stuart: They put me to bed when I'm wide awake and wake me up when I'm fast asleep.

My mum is extravagant with her clothes. When she has a new dress she wears it out the first day.

What did the little light bulb say to its mum?
'I wuv you watts and watts.'

Mum: From now on you're going to have free school dinners.
Sarah: But, Mum, I don't want three school dinners, one is more than enough.

Big Sister: I can marry anyone I please.
Little Sister: But you don't please anyone.

Don't look out of the window, Mum. People will think it's Halloween.

My mum went on a banana diet. She didn't lose any weight, but she can't half climb trees well.

Mum: You're late for school. Have you got your socks on yet?
Tom: Yes, Mum. All except one.

Mum: Why are you eating so fast?
Tom: I don't want to lose my appetite.

Sarah: Mum, is it true that my baby brother came
from heaven?
Mum: Yes.
Sarah: I can see why God threw him out.

Jamie: Where does your mum come from?
Sarah: Alaska.
Jamie: No, it's all right, I'll ask her myself.

We're so poor that Mum and Dad can't afford to
buy me shoes. I have to polish my feet and lace my
toes together.

What's old, pink and wrinkled and belongs to
Grandma?
Grandpa.

Mum and Dad are in the iron and steel business. She
does the ironing and he does the stealing.

Mum: What do you think of this photograph of me?
Dad: It makes you look older.
Mum: Oh, well, it'll save the cost of having another
one taken later on.

Mother: How was your first day at school?
Sarah: OK, but I haven't got my present yet.
Mother: What do you mean?
Sarah: Well, the teacher gave me a chair and said,
'Sit there for the present.'

Tom: Dad, will you do my homework for me?
Dad: No, son. It wouldn't be right.
Tom: It wouldn't be right if I did it either.

Mum: I went to an art exhibition today.
Dad: Gaugin?
Mum: No, once was plenty.

Sarah: Mum, how much pocket money can I have?
Mum: Ten pence a week.
Sarah: Ten pence. That's an insult.
Mum: In that case, I'll give it to you monthly so you won't feel insulted so often.

Sophie: How is your mum getting on with her diet?
Sarah: Very well. She's almost disappeared.

My mum made me a lovely birthday cake but there was one problem: the candles melted in the oven.

Mum, your cooking is improving. Now the smoke in the kitchen is grey rather than black.

Mum: Did you miss me while I was away?
Dad: Oh, have you been away?

What is the cheapest time to call your family long distance?
When they're not home.

Jamie: Mum, you have the face of a saint.
Mum: Thank you. Which one?
Jamie: Saint Bernard.

Tom: Mum, can I have fifty pence for being good?
Mum: All right, but I wish you could be good-for-nothing.

Jenny: How did Mum know that you hadn't had a bath?
Stuart: I forgot to splash water on the floor.

Dad: My hair is getting thinner.
Mum: Who wants fat hair anyway?

My sister sent her photograph off to a Lonely Hearts club. They sent it back saying that they weren't that lonely!

Sophie: How awful that your aunt drowned in a tub of varnish.
Louisa: Yes, but what a finish.

Jane: Mum, do you know what I'm going to give you for your birthday?
Mum: No, dear, what?
Jane: A nice teapot.
Mum: But I've got a nice teapot.
Jane: No you haven't. I've just dropped it.

Who is bigger, Mr Bigger or Mr Bigger's baby?
The baby is a little Bigger.

Mum: Did you meet your father at the station?
Tom: No, silly. I've known him all my life.

Jamie: My dad went on a crash diet this week.
Tom: Is that why he looks such a wreck?

My dad is so old, when he was at school, history was called current events.

Jenny: How did you do in your exams?
Stuart: I did what Napoleon did.
Jenny: What was that?
Stuart: Went down in history.

Louisa: Mummy, does God use our bathroom?
Mum: No.
Louisa: Then why does Daddy beat the door and say, 'Oh God. Are you still in there?'

My dad's idea of housework is to sweep the room
with a glance.

My dad is so short sighted he can't get to sleep
unless he counts elephants.

Sarah: Why does your dad keep a ruler on his
newspaper?
Sophie: Because he likes to get his story straight.

Dad: I'm very disappointed in you. Why is your
January report card so bad?
Jamie: You know how it is, Dad. Everything gets
marked down after Christmas.

Tom: Dad, can I have a new pair of trainers for gym, please?
Dad: Why can't Jim buy his own?

Sophie: What sort of car has your dad got?
Sarah: I can't remember the name. I think it starts with T.
Sophie: Really? Ours only starts with petrol.

Tom: Mum, you know that vase that's been handed down from generation to generation?
Mum: Yes.
Tom: Well, this generation's dropped it.

My granny had so many candles on her birthday cake, we were driven back by the heat.

My dad used to be a sailor but he was discharged from the submarine service. He was caught sleeping with the windows open.

Dad: Oh no, I just went through a red light.
Louisa: That's all right Dad, the police car behind you just did the same thing.

Dad's gravy is so thick, when I try to stir it, the house spins around.

My dad is so stupid he got fired from his job as a lift attendant. He couldn't remember the route.

Dad: How are your grades, son?
Jamie: Under water, Dad.
Dad: Under water? What do you mean?
Jamie: They're below C level.

My dad gets called into school so often that he has a better attendance record than me.

Dad: When I was your age I thought nothing of walking five miles to school.
Tom: I don't think much of it myself.

Tom: Dad, there's a man at the door collecting for the new swimming pool.
Dad: Give him a glass of water.

Dad: How many times have I told you to stop playing with my calculator?
Sophie: 252,345.266666

Sarah: Mum, do you think I should take up the piano as a career?
Mum: No, I think you should put down the lid as a favour.

My dad works in a watch factory. He sits around all day making faces.

Tom: Do you have a good memory for faces, Dad?
Dad: Yes, why?
Tom: Because I've just broken your shaving mirror.

Sophie: What does your dad put on his carrots?
Jamie: Cow manure.
Sophie: I prefer a little butter.

Jamie: Dad, would you like to save some money?
Dad: I certainly would, son. Any suggestions?
Jamie: Why not buy me a bike, then I won't wear my shoes out so fast.

I wouldn't say my dad's thick headed but he's the only person I know who's allowed to ride a motorbike without a helmet.

My dad is so lazy that he sticks his nose out of the window so that the wind will blow it for him.

Mum: Where's this morning's newspaper?
Louisa: I wrapped the rubbish in it and threw it out.
Mum: But I wanted to see it.
Louisa: There wasn't much to see. Only some bacon rinds, two egg shells and some tea bags.

Dad: This report gives you a D for conduct and an A for courtesy. How did you manage that?
Tom: Easy. Whenever I punch someone, I apologise.

Jamie: Dad, where's the English Channel?
Dad: You know we don't have digital TV.

My dad just got booked for speeding. The policeman said that he was doing ninety miles per hour, but my dad said he'd only been in the car for ten minutes.

Dad: Didn't you hear me hammering on your bedroom door last night?
Jamie: Oh, that's OK, Dad, I was playing my music very loud so you didn't disturb me.

Dad: I think our daughter got her brains from me.
Mum: She must have, because I've still got mine.

My dad started at the top and worked his way down. He's a deep sea diver.

What did the bald dad say when he got a comb for his birthday?
'Thanks, I'll never part with it.'

Dad: How did the greenhouse get smashed?
Jamie: I was cleaning my catapult and it went off.

Dad: I'll cook you dinner. What would you like?
Mum: An insurance policy.

No one could call my dad a quitter. He's been sacked
from every job he's ever had.

Tom: Dad, how much am I worth to you?
Dad: A million pounds, son.
Tom: In that case, can I borrow a fiver?

Dad: You shouldn't hit a boy when he's down.
Jamie: What do you think I got him down for?

Mum: Who's at the door?
Sophie: A man with a drum.
Mum: Tell him to beat it.

Sarah: My dad owns a newspaper.
Sophie: Big deal. They only cost thirty pence.

Tom: My dad hates to see my mum work herself into the ground.
Sophie: What does he do?
Tom: He draws the curtains and watches telly.

Yesterday my dad had to get a potato clock. That's so he could be in the office by eight-thirty.

Tom: Dad, are you superstitious?
Dad: No, son.
Tom: Then will you lend me £13?

Mum: Why is your sister crying?
Holly: Because I won't give her one of my crisps.
Mum: Well, what has she done with her own crisps?
Holly: She cried when I ate them, too.

My dad has such a big mouth, he can sing a duet by himself.

Mum: Be sure that you go straight to school.
Louisa: I can't, it's round the corner.

My dad is rather tired this morning. Last night he dreamed he was working.

Dad: I'm just going out to water the garden.
Mum: But it's raining
Dad: It's OK, I'll take an umbrella.

Sarah: Dad, what are you giving Mum for Christmas?
Dad: A list of what I want.

'My dad is so lazy that when he drops something he waits till he has to tie his shoelaces before he'll pick it up.'

My dad has so many wrinkles he has to screw his hat on.

Dad: Have you been fighting again? You've lost your front teeth.
Tom: No, I haven't. They're in my pocket.

Dad: Who broke my shaver?
Jamie: I don't know. It was still working last night when I used it to sharpen my pencil.

Tom: My sister should have been born in the Dark Ages.
Jamie: Why?
Tom: She looks awful in daylight.

Jane: Mum, is it true that people spring from dust?
Mum: Yes.
Jane: In that case, look under my bed and you'll witness the birth of a nation.

GOOFY GAMES

How long does it take to learn to roller skate?
A hundred sittings.

What do you win if you come fourth in a race for worried people?
A consternation prize.

Why are fish rotten tennis players?
They don't like getting close to the net.

What do you call fishing when you don't catch any fish?
Drowning worms.

Did you hear about the stupid athlete who bought a book called How to Hurdle?
When he got home he found it was volume seven of an encyclopedia.

What creepy crawlies do athletes break?
Tapeworms.

Stuart: Let's play a game of wits.
Jenny: No, let's play something you can join in with.

Stuart: Can you roller skate?
Jenny: I don't know. I've never been able to stand up long enough to find out.

Why did the forgetful elephant take up running?
To jog his memory.

What happens if you play table tennis with a bad egg?
First it goes ping, then it goes pong.

Why was the ball dribbling?
You'd dribble too if your head was bouncing off the floor.

Joe: What happened to you?
Sandra: I fell while I was riding.
Joe: Horseback?
Sandra: I don't know. I'll find out when I get back to the barn.

What's the world's longest punctuation mark?
The fifty yard dash.

Why did the soccer player kick his computer?
He wanted to boot up the system.

What's the best animal to take along when you go swimming?
A giraft.

What is a mosquito's favourite sport?
Skin-diving.

Jeanette: Are you going to watch the rugby international this afternoon?
Bob: No, it's a waste of time. I can tell you the score before the game starts.
Jeanette: Can you? What is it then?
Bob: Nil nil.

How did Pinocchio win all his races?
By a nose.

It is well known that exercise kills germs.
But how do you get the germs to exercise?

Michelle: Why are you putting the saddle on backwards?
Mark: How do you know which way I'm going?

Spaniard: The national sport in Spain is bullfighting and in England it's cricket.
Englishman: I'd rather play in England.
Spaniard: Why is that?
Englishman: It's easier to fight crickets.

What athlete is never promoted?
The left back.

How do you service your pogo stick?
Give it a spring clean.

What is a vampire's favourite sport?
Drac racing.

What do you win if you come fourth in a race in a graveyard?
A consecration prize.

What is a cross-channel swimmer's favourite song?
'Please Re-grease Me.'

Where do zombies play golf?
On the golf corpse.

What is the quietest game?
Tenpin bowling, because you can hear a pin drop.

What game do wizard octopi play?
Squidditch.

Captain: Why didn't you stop that ball?
Goalie: That's what the net's for, isn't it?

When is cricket a crime?
When there's a hit and run.

Why couldn't the car play football?
Because it only had one boot.

What should a football team do if the pitch is flooded?
Bring on their subs.

If you have a referee in football, and an umpire in tennis, what do you have in bowls?
Goldfish.

Which athlete is the warmest?
A long jumper.

Which birds are batsmen most frightened of?
Ducks.

When was cricket first mentioned in the Bible?
In the first line: 'in the big inning'.

Why did the midfield player refuse to travel by
aeroplane?
He didn't want to be put on the wing.

What's an owl's favourite sport?
Hootball.

What's the chilliest ground in the Premiership?
Cold Trafford.

A manager is talking to his team before a big game.
'Now come on lads,' he says, 'we need to win this so
that I can have the cash to buy some new players.'

What do you call a bunch of chess players bragging
in a hotel lobby at Christmas?
Chess nuts boasting in an open foyer.

How did the football pitch end up as a triangle?
Somebody took a corner.

A marathon runner ran for three hours but only
moved two feet. How come?
He only had two feet.

What do you get if you drop a piano on a team's
defence?
A flat back four.

What goes in pink and comes out again blue?
A swimmer in winter.

First crossword fan: I've been trying to think of a
word for two weeks.
Second crossword fan: How about a fortnight?

What happens to a footballer when his eyesight starts to fail?
He becomes a referee.

If it takes ten sportsmen half an hour to eat a ham, how long will it take twenty sportsmen to eat half a ham?
It depends whether they're professionals or 'am-a-chewers.

What soccer team do snakes support?
Slitherpool.

Why can't zebras play football?
Because they've got two left feet.

What's the hardest part about learning to skate?
The ice.

Did you hear about the idiot who won the Tour de France?
He did a lap of honour.

First trampolinist: How's life?
Second trampolinist: Oh, up and down, you know.

If you have a referee in football and an umpire in cricket, what do you have in bowls?
Trifle.

HARE-
BRAINED
HISTORY

Who ruled France until he exploded?
Napoleon Blownapart.

Why couldn't prehistoric man send birthday cards?
The stamps kept falling off the rocks.

How did the Romans brush their cats?
With catacombs.

Why did the mummy leave his tomb after 3,000 years?
Because he thought he was old enough to leave home.

Who was the greatest comedian in the Bible?
Samson – he brought the house down.

What followed the dinosaurs?
Their tails.

What was the speed limit in Ancient Egypt?
Sixty Niles an hour.

Why does history give you the runs?
Because it's full of dates.

What did Caesar say after Brutus stabbed him?
'Ouch.'

Did they play tennis in ancient Egypt?
Yes, the Bible tells how Joseph served in Pharoah's court.

Jamie: One of my ancestors died at Waterloo.
Sarah: Really, which platform?

Which kings and queens are not buried in Westminster Abbey?
The ones that aren't dead yet.

What is the famous skunk statue in Egypt?
The Stinx.

A dad was reading a Bible story to his young son. He read:
'Lot was warned to take his wife and flee out of the city but his wife looked back and was turned to salt.' His son asked, 'What happened to the flea?'

How many apostles can you fit in a car?
All of them. It says in the Bible that 'they met in one Accord'.

Was Noah the first one out of the Ark?
No, he came forth out of the ark.

Which mouse was a Roman emperor?
Julius Cheeser.

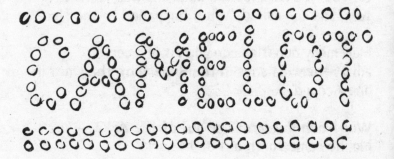

What was Camelot famous for?
Its knight life.

What does the Queen do when she burps?
Issues a royal pardon.

Why was Christopher Columbus a crook?
Because he double-crossed the Atlantic.

What is a forum?
Two-um plus two-um.

Noah: I thought we had two turkeys when we left.
Mrs Noah: Well, it is Christmas.

Why does history keep repeating itself?
Because we weren't listening the first time.

Ugly lady: That painting you did of me doesn't do me justice.
Picasso: It's not justice you want, it's mercy.

How do we know the Romans were brainy?
They could all speak Latin.

Who was round and shiny and invaded England?
William the Conker.

Which Ancient Egyptian king was good at washing-up?
Pharaoh Liquid.

Who succeeded the first Prime Minister?
The second one.

What does 1286 BC inscribed on the mummy's tomb
indicate?
The registration of the car that ran him over.

Which civilisation invented the fountain pen?
The Incas.

How do we know that Rome was built at night?
Because it wasn't built in a day.

What kind of lights did Noah put on the ark?
Floodlights.

Who had a big nose and invaded England?
William the Conk.

Name one of Noah's children.
Joan of Ark.

Did you hear about the stupid inventor who created the one-piece jigsaw puzzle?

Stuart: You remind me of a Greek statue.
Jenny: Do you mean you think I'm beautiful?
Stuart: Yes, beautiful, but not all there.

What happened to Abel when he died?
He became un-Abel.

Where was Solomon's temple?
On the side of his head.

Why did the Romans build straight roads?
Because their horses didn't have steering wheels.

How do you use an Ancient Egyptian doorbell?
Toot-and-come-in.

Why did King Arthur jump up and down and ask for
a tin opener?
He had ants in his armour.

What did Adam do when he wanted some sugar?
He raised Cain.

Who made King Arthur's round table?
Sir Cumference.

Who is the fastest prime minister ever?
Tony Blur.

Which English king brewed his own wine?
Alfred the Grape.

Where was Henry VIII crowned?
On his head.

What was Noah's job?
He was an ark-itect.

Why do pirates do the sword dance?
So they can dance and cut their toenails at the
same time.

What was the most popular instrument in British
history?
The Anglosaxophone.

Which king was always drunk?
Richard the Slurred.

Which king liked drinking smoothies?
Edward the Compressor.

Why did Henry VIII have so many wives?
He liked to chop and change.

What did the dragon say when he met a knight in shining armour?
I love tinned food.

Which English queen liked gambling?
Mary Queen of Slots.

How was the Roman Empire divided?
With a pair of Caesars.

Caesar: What's the weather like?
Brutus: Hail, Caesar.

How do we know the Romans invented soap?
Because they created the Holy Foaming Empire.

'Has anyone ever told you you look like Robbie
Williams?'
'No.'
'It doesn't surprise me. You don't.'

Which king had a mobile phone?
William of Orange.

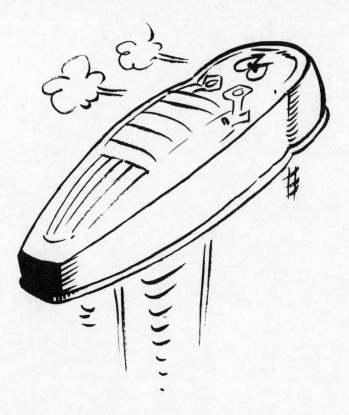

How can you tell when a mummy is angry?
He flips his lid.

What was Noah's occupation?
Preserving pairs.

Adam was naming the animals. 'This,' he said to Eve,
'is a giraffe.'
'Why do you call it a giraffe?' asked Eve.
'Because it looks like a giraffe, stupid.'

KNOCK KNOCK

Knock, knock.
Who's there?
Roach.
Roach who?
Roach out and touch someone.

Knock, knock.
Who's there?
Water.
Water who?
Water you answering the door for?

Knock, knock.
Who's there?
Ammonia.
Ammonia who?
Ammonia a bird in a gilded cage.

Knock, knock.
Who's there?
Madam.
Madam who?
Madam foot is caught in the door.

Knock, knock.
Who's there?
Goat.
Goat who?
Goat to the door and find out!

Knock, knock.
Who's there?
Aware.
Aware who?
Aware, aware has my little dog gone?

Knock, knock.
Who's there?
Luck.
Luck who?
Luck through the keyhole and you'll find out.

Knock, knock.
Who's there?
Oliver.
Oliver who?
Oliver cross the road from you!

Knock, knock.
Who's there?
Repeat.
Repeat who?
Who, who, who.

Knock, knock.
Who's there?
Dot.
Dot who?
Dots for me to know, and you to find out.

Knock, knock.
Who's there?
Archie.
Archie Who?
Bless you!

Knock, knock.
Who's there?
I used.
I used who?
I used to be able to reach the doorbell, but now I can't!

Knock, knock.
Who's there?
Butch and Jimmy.
Butch and Jimmy who?
Butch your arms around me and Jimmy a kiss!

Knock, knock.
Who's there?
Dime.
Dime who?
Dime to come in.

Knock, knock.
Who's there?
Never.
Never who?
Never mind.

Knock, knock.
Who's there?
Argue.
Argue who?
Argue going to let me in?

Knock, knock.
Who's there?
Ben.
Ben who?
Ben over and kiss me!

Knock, knock.
Who's there?
Cash.
Cash who?
No, thanks I'm allergic to nuts.

Knock, knock.
Who's there?
Value.
Value who?
Value let me in?

Knock, knock.
Who's there?
Radio.
Radio who?
Radio not, here I come!

Knock, knock.
Who's there?
Dishes.
Dishes who?
Dishes me. Who ish you?

Knock, knock.
Who's there?
Yule.
Yule who?
Yule never know!

Knock, knock.
Who's there?
I-8.
I-8 who?
I-8 to trouble you, but can I stay the night?

Knock, knock.
Who's there?
Scott.
Scott who?
Scott nothing to do with you.

Knock, knock.
Who's there?
Hal.
Hal who?
Hal who to you too!

Knock, knock.
Who's there?
Beefst.
Beefst who?
Yes please, I'm starving!

Knock, knock.
Who's there?
Tads.
Tads who?
Tads not important.

Knock, knock.
Who's there?
Do-wap.
Do-wap who?
No thanks, I've just been.

Knock, knock.
Who's there?
Toogle.
Toogle who?
Oh, are you leaving already?

Knock, knock.
Who's there?
Tree.
Tree who?
Tree blind mice.

Knock, knock.
Who's there?
Baby.
Baby who?
Baby I'll come back later.

Knock, knock.
Who's there?
Window wind.
Window wind who?
Window wind blows, the cradle will rock.

Knock, knock.
Who's there?
Gary.
Gary who?
Gary the can.

Knock, knock.
Who's there?
Juicy.
Juicy who?
Juicy what I see?

Knock, knock.
Who's there?
Keith.
Keith who?
Keith your hands off me!

Knock, knock.
Who's there?
Maida.
Maida who?
Maida cake and thought you'd like some.

Knock, knock.
Who's there?
Major.
Major who?
Major open the door!

Knock, knock.
Who's there?
Camera.
Camera who?
Camera come in?

Knock, knock.
Who's there?
Beetroot.
Beetroot who?
Beetroot to yourself.

Knock, knock.
Who's there?
Toucan.
Toucan who?
Toucan play at that game.

Knock, knock.
Who's there?
Buddha.
Buddha who?
Buddha kettle on.

Knock, knock.
Who's there?
Wallet.
Wallet who?
Wallet rain this afternoon?

Knock, knock.
Who's there?
Oswald.
Oswald who?
Oswald my chewing gum.

KOOKY CLASSES

Louisa: Mum, you know you're always worried about me failing maths?
Mum: Yes.
Louisa: Well, your worries are over.

Teacher: Name three famous poles.
Stuart: North, South and Tad.

Teacher: Did you have help with your homework?
Pupil: No, I got it wrong all by myself.

Teacher: Sarah, are you sleeping in my class?
Sarah: Not any more, Miss.

Teacher: What's the difference between ignorance and apathy?
James: I don't know and I don't care.

Teacher: Tom, define 'artery'.
Tom: It's the study of paintings.

Why did the teacher jump into the lake?
Because she wanted to test the water.

Teacher: What does 'coincidence' mean?
Richard: Funny, I was going to ask you the same thing.

Teacher: James, what does your father do?
James: Whatever my mum tells him to.

Teacher: Where is your essay on time travel?
Pupil: I haven't done it yet, Miss, but I promise I'll hand it in yesterday.

Teacher: What's your name?
Pupil: Richard Mickey O'Toole.
Teacher: I'll call you Richard O'Toole for short.
Pupil: I'd rather you didn't take the Mickey out of my name.

Teacher: Who was the Roman queen of the gods?
Pupil: Juno.
Teacher: Yes, but I'm asking you.

Teacher: What did your parents say about your school report?
Pupil: Shall I leave out the bad language?
Teacher: Of course.
Pupil: In that case, they didn't say anything.

Mum: Do you know a girl named Jenny?
Louisa: Yes, she sleeps next to me in Maths.

Teacher: Spell 'horse'.
Jimmy: H, O, R, S.
Teacher: And what comes at the end?
Jimmy: Its tail, Miss.

Teacher: How fast does light travel?
Paul: I don't know, but it always arrives too early in the morning.

Teacher: Jamie, wipe that mud off your shoes before you come in the classroom.
Jamie: But, Sir, I'm not wearing any shoes.

Did you hear about the brilliant geography teacher?
He had abroad knowledge of his subject.

Teacher: Name the four seasons.
Sophie: Salt, pepper, mustard and vinegar.

Teacher: You look pale today, Tom.
Tom: I think I must have overwashed.

Sophie: Our teacher talks to herself, does yours?
Sarah: Yes, but she doesn't realise it; she thinks we're actually listening.

Teacher: In this exam you will be allowed ten minutes for each question.
Pupil: How long is the answer?

Teacher: What's the matter, Oliver?
Oliver (the school swot): I'm a bit worried.
Teacher: Tense?
Oliver: I am a bit worried, I was a bit worried, I will be a bit worried, I will have been a bit worried.

Pupil: How do you spell ichaelangelo?
Teacher: Don't you mean Michaelangelo?
Pupil: No, Miss, I've written the 'M' already.

Why shouldn't you bring your pet piranha to class?
Because they attack in schools.

Teacher: Who was the first woman on earth?
Jenny: I don't know, Sir.
Teacher: Come on, Jenny, it has something to do with an apple.
Jenny: Granny Smith?

Teacher: What are you writing?
Pupil: A letter to myself.
Teacher: What does it say?
Pupil: I don't know. I won't get it till tomorrow.

Teacher: Today we're studying percentages. If there are ten questions on a quiz and you get ten correct, what do you get?
Pupil: Accused of cheating.

Teacher: Sophie, your homework looks as if it is in your father's handwriting.
Sophie: Well, I used his pen, Miss.

Teacher: How many books did you finish over the summer?
Stuart: None. My brother stole my box of crayons.

Our school librarian is very strict. She'll send you to the head teacher's office for thinking too loudly.

Teacher: You aren't paying attention to me. Are you having trouble hearing?
Pupil: No, Sir, I'm having trouble listening.

Teacher: How many books have you read in your lifetime?
Pupil: I don't know. I'm not dead yet.

Teacher: Tom, name three collective nouns.
Tom: The wastepaper basket, the wheely bin and the vacuum cleaner.

Teacher: What do you call a person who keeps on talking when people are no longer interested?
Pupil: A teacher.

Teacher: Jamie, what is the climate of New Zealand?
Jamie: Very cold, Sir.
Teacher: Wrong.
Jamie: But Sir, when they send us meat, it always arrives frozen.

Teacher: I told you to write this poem out twenty times because your handwriting is so bad.
Sarah: I'm sorry Miss – my arithmetic's not that good either.

Teacher: Now class, whatever I ask, I want you to all answer at once. How much is six plus four?
Class: At once.

Why did the children eat their homework?
Because the teacher said it was a piece of cake.

I'm so bad at Art, my teacher says it is a wonder I can draw breath.

Jane: How come you did so badly in history? I thought you had all the dates written on your sleeve?
Louisa: That's the trouble, I put on my geography blouse by mistake.

Teacher: Sophie, why are you doing your sums on the floor?
Sophie: You told me to do it without using tables.

Teacher: That's an excellent essay for someone your age.
Tom: How about for someone my dad's age, Miss?

Teacher: Jamie, give me two pronouns.
Jamie: Who, me?
Teacher: Correct!

Mum: How did you do in the grammar test?
Jamie: Great, Mum. I only made one mistake and I seen it as soon as I done it.

Father: I want to remove my daughter from this terrible maths class.
Teacher: But she's top of the class.
Father: That's why I think it must be a terrible class.

Teacher: What are the Great Plains?
Pupil: 747, Concorde and F-16.

Music student: Did you really learn to play the violin in six easy lessons?
Music teacher: Yes, but the 500 that followed were pretty tough.

Head teacher: I hear you missed school yesterday.
Tom: Not a bit.

Teacher: Class, we will have only half a day of school this morning.
Class: Hooray.
Teacher: We will have the other half this afternoon.

Teacher: An abstract noun is something you can think of, but you can't touch it. Can you give me an example of one?
Jamie: My father's new car.

Teacher: Define 'procrastination'.
Pupil: Can I do it tomorrow?

Teacher: Why don't you write more neatly?
Sarah: So you can't spot my terrible spelling.

Teacher: Sophie, use the word 'income' in a sentence.
Sophie: 'I opened the door and income the dog.'
Teacher: No, no. Try the word 'ransom'.
Sophie: 'I saw a skunk and ransom distance to get away.'

Art teacher: And what are you drawing Louisa?
Louisa: Heaven, Miss.
Art teacher: But no one knows what heaven looks like.
Louisa: They will when I've finished, won't they?

Teacher: How many days of the week start with the letter T?
Tom: Tuesday, Thursday, today and tomorrow.

Teacher: Give me a sentence with the word 'gruesome'.
Sophie: 'I wasn't very tall last year but since then I gruesome.'

Teacher: Did the Native Americans hunt bear?
Jamie: Not in the winter.

Teacher: Who started the fight?
Pupil: He did, Miss. He purposely hit me back.

Teacher: What is a 'duchess'?
Louisa: It's the same as an English 's'.

Teacher: How can I get you to devote as much
energy to your class work as you devote to break?
Pupil: Start playing football in class.

Teacher: Simon, can you spell your name
backwards?
Simon: Nomis.

Teacher: Why are you always late?
Jamie: I threw away my alarm clock.
Teacher: But why?
Jamie: Because it always goes off when I'm asleep.

Mum: Did you get a good place in the geography test?
Tom: Yes, Mum. I sat next to the cleverest kid in the class.

Teacher: Why are you late for school?
Sophie: I had to say goodbye to my pets.
Teacher: But you're two hours late.
Sophie: I keep bees.

Why did the teacher take a ruler to bed?
Because he wanted to see how long he slept.

When can school uniforms be a fire hazard?
When they are blazers.

Stuart: I'm not going back to school ever again.
Jenny: Why ever not?
Stuart: The teacher doesn't know a thing; all she
does is ask questions.

Teacher: What would you do if I came to school
with a face as dirty as yours, Stuart?
Stuart: Nothing Miss, I'm too polite.

Teacher: How do they predict rainstorms when the weather satellites fail?
Jamie: They ask my dad when he's going to wash his car.

Teacher: What does your history book tell you about the Civil War?
Pupil: It doesn't tell me anything. I have to read it.

Dad: How were the exam questions?
Tom: Easy.
Dad: Then why look so unhappy?
Tom: The questions were easy, but the answers were impossible.

Teacher: How far are you from getting the right answer?
Pupil: Two seats.

What's a teacher's favourite country?
Expla-nation.

What did you learn in school today?
Not enough, I have to go back tomorrow.

Pupil (on phone): My son has a bad cold and won't be able to come to school today.
School secretary: Who is this?
Pupil: This is my father speaking.

One kid in our class gets in a fight every day after school. He says it helps keep him out of trouble.

Teacher: Sophie, tell me a sentence with 'geometry' in it.
Sophie: 'The acorn went to sleep for a long time and when he woke up he said "gee, I'm a tree."'

Teacher: Why haven't you studied your geography?
Stuart: Well, my dad says the world is changing every day. So I'm going to wait till it settles down.

Teacher: Why were you late for school?
Stuart: Well, there are eight of us in our family and the alarm was set for seven.

My teacher says our schoolbooks are a magic carpet that will take us all over the world. I took mine to the garage and had them fitted with seat belts.

Geography teacher: How can you prove that the world is round?
Jamie: But I never said it was, Sir.

Teacher: If your father earned £1,000 a week and gave you half, what would you have?
Tom: A heart attack.

Pupil: I don't think I deserve zero for this paper.
Teacher: Neither do I, but it's the lowest grade I can give you.

Dad: I hear you skipped school to play football.
Jamie: No I didn't, and I have the fish to prove it.

Why are some whales at the bottom of the ocean?
Because they dropped out of school.

Teacher: I'd like to go through one whole day
without having to tell you off.
Jamie: You have my permission.

Mum: What did you learn in school today?
Louisa: How to write.
Mum: What did you write?
Louisa: I don't know; they haven't taught us how to
read yet.

Teacher: What happened to your homework?
Pupil: I made it into a paper plane and someone
hijacked it.

Teacher: Don't whistle while you're studying.
Tom: I'm not studying. I'm just whistling.

Teacher: Why can't you answer any of my questions?
Pupil: Well if I could there wouldn't be much point in me being here.

Teacher: Can you give an example of a 'coincidence'?
Sophie: Yes, Miss: my mum and dad got married on the same day and at the same time.

Chemistry teacher: Name a liquid that won't freeze.
Jamie: Hot water.

What's yellow, has wheels and lies on its back?
A dead school bus.

Teacher: Why have you got a sausage stuck behind your ear?
Jamie: Oh, no, I must have eaten my pencil for lunch.

What are a teacher's three favourite words?
June, July and August.

Is a hammer a good tool for maths?
No, you need multi-pliers.

Teacher: Can anyone tell me how many seconds there are in a year?
Sophie: Twelve: 2nd January, 2nd February . . .

Teacher: Well, at least there's one thing I can say about your son.
Father: What's that?
Teacher: With grades like his, he couldn't be cheating.

Teacher: What is the chemical formula for water?
Jamie: HIJKLMNO.
Teacher: What are you talking about?
Jamie: Yesterday you said it's H to O.

Teacher: Are you homesick?
Louisa: No, I'm here sick.

What do elves learn in school?
The Elf-abet.

Mum: How did you enjoy your first day at school, Jamie?
Jamie: First day? You mean I have to go back there tomorrow?

History teacher: Sophie, would you have liked to live in Tudor times?
Sophie: Oh, yes, Sir. I'd have loved it.
History teacher: Why?
Sophie: Because I would have had 500 years less history to learn.

English teacher: Give me a sentence using the word 'fascinate'.
Sophie: 'My raincoat has ten buttons but I can only fasten eight.'

Teacher: If I gave you two rabbits on Monday and three rabbits on Tuesday and four rabbits on Wednesday, how many rabbits would you have?
Pupil: Ten. I've got one already.

What did the maths textbook say to the reading textbook?
'Don't tell me your sad stories, I'm the one with the problems.'

My teacher has a sympathetic face. Every time I see her I feel sympathy for her.

Teacher: You must have a sixth sense.
Pupil: Why, Sir?
Teacher: Because you show no signs of having the other five.

Teacher: If there were five magpies in a tree and the farmer shot one, how many would be left?
Pupil: None, Miss, they'd have all flown away.

Art teacher: I asked you to draw a horse and trap. You've only drawn the horse.
Jamie: Well, Sir. I thought the horse would draw the trap.

Teacher: Sarah, didn't you hear me call you?
Sarah: Yes, Miss, but you told us yesterday not to answer back.

Teacher: Didn't you promise to behave?
Pupil: Yes, Sir.
Teacher: And didn't I promise to punish you if you didn't?
Pupil: Yes, Sir, but since I broke my promise, I don't expect you to keep yours.

Teacher: What came after the Stone Age and the Bronze Age?
Pupil: The sausage.

Teacher: Tom, I hope I didn't see you looking at Louisa's work then.
Tom: So do I, Miss.

Teacher: Sophie, give me a sentence starting with 'I'.
Sophie: 'I is –'
Teacher: No, Sophie. Always say, 'I am'.
Sophie: OK. 'I am the ninth letter of the alphabet.'

What's a mushroom?
The place they store the school food.

Brian: I don't want to go to school today, Mum. I hate it.
Mum: You must go dear. You're the head teacher.

Pupil: Miss, I'm going to be really lazy this term.
Teacher: Why? Hard work never killed anyone.
Pupil: I know, and I don't plan to be its first victim.

Teacher: Name six things that contain milk.
Sophie: Cheese, ice cream and four cows.

Teacher: I said to draw a cow eating some grass but you've drawn nothing.
Jamie: Well, the cow ate all the grass.
Teacher: So where's the cow?
Jamie: It's gone to another field where there's more grass.

Teacher: Why are you late?
Louisa: Because of that sign.
Teacher: What sign?
Louisa: The one that says, 'School Ahead, Go Slow'.

Teacher: Sophie, your spelling has certainly improved. There are only six mistakes here.
Sophie: Oh good.
Teacher: Now let's look at the second line, shall we?

Teacher: Why are you always late to class?
Pupil: Because you always ring the bell before I get here.

Teacher: If 'can't' is short for 'cannot', what is 'don't' short for?
Pupil: Doughnut.

Teacher: Tell the class what book you read and then tell them something about the plot.

Sarah: I read The Life of Napoleon. He dies at the end.

Mum: Why did you get such a low mark on that test?

Tom: Because of absence.

Mum: You mean you were absent on the day of the test?

Tom: No, but the boy who sits next to me was.

How do Religious Education teachers mark exams? With spirit levels.

Teacher: You can't bring that sheep into school.
What about the smell?
Bo Peep: Oh, that's all right, it'll soon get used to it.

Did you hear about the maths teacher who fainted
in class?
Everyone tried to bring her two.

Sophie: Dad, can you write in the dark?
Dad: I think so. What do you want me to write?
Sophie: Your name on this report card.

Louisa: My teacher's a peach.
Mum: You mean she's sweet.
Louisa: No, she has a heart of stone.

Teacher: What is the plural of mouse?
Sophie: Mice.
Teacher: And what is the plural of baby?
Sophie: Twins.

Mum: Why did you swallow the money I gave you?
Louisa: You said it was my lunch money.

What's black and white all over and difficult?
An exam paper.

What kind of food do maths teachers eat?
Square meals.

Jamie: I think our school has a ghost in it.
Tom: Why?
Jamie: Because our head teacher is always talking about our school spirit.

Maths teacher: What's two plus two?
Jamie: Four.
Maths teacher: That's good.
Jamie: Good? That's perfect.

Teacher: Why does the Statue of Liberty stand in New York harbour?
Pupil: Because it can't sit down.

Teacher: If 1+1=2 and 2+2=4, what is 4+4?
Jamie: That's not fair. You answer the easy ones and leave us with the hard one.

Teacher: Where is your homework?
Tom: I lost it fighting this kid who said you weren't the best teacher in the school.

Dad: Why aren't you doing very well in history?
Sophie: Because the teacher keeps asking about things that happened before I was born.

Science teacher: Name me a deadly poison.
Jenny: Tightrope walking.
Science teacher: That's not a poison.
Jenny: Well, one drop and you've had it.

Teacher: I asked you to write an essay about milk and you have only written two lines. Why?
Jane: I'm writing about condensed milk.

Teacher: Now Stuart, do you understand how important punctuation is?
Stuart: Yes. That's why I always arrive at school on time.

Teacher: Sarah, this essay about your pet dog is word for word the same one your brother handed in.
Sarah: Yes, Miss. It's the same dog.

Stuart: My teacher said we are having a test today, rain or shine.
Mum: Then why are you so happy?
Stuart: It's snowing.

Teacher: How many seasons are there in a year?
Stuart: Two Sir: cricket and football.

Teacher: If I cut two apples and two bananas into ten pieces each, and then add ten cherries, what do I have?
Tom: A fruit salad.

Teacher: Use the word 'climate' in a sentence.
Sophie: 'I have an apple tree in my garden but my parents won't let me climate.'

Teacher: Jane, you copied from Louisa's test didn't you?
Jane: How did you find out?
Teacher: Louisa's answer says, 'I don't know,' and yours says, 'Me neither'.

Teacher: Why do you always get so dirty?
Jamie: Well, I'm a lot closer to the ground than you are.

Lollypop lady: Jamie, why are you trying to cross the road here? There's a zebra crossing fifty yards up the road.
Jamie: Well, I hope it's having more luck than me.

Head teacher: Sophie, you should have been here half an hour ago.
Sophie: Why, what happened?

Teacher: Recite your tables to me, Stuart.
Stuart: Dining table, kitchen table, bedside table . . .

Mum: How are you doing in arithmetic?
Sophie: I've learned to add up the zeros, but the numbers are still giving me trouble.

Teacher: If I lay one egg here and another there, how many eggs will there be?
Tom: None.
Teacher: Why not?
Tom: Because you can't lay eggs.

Louisa: I've added these figures ten times.
Teacher: Good work.
Louisa: And here are my ten answers.

Dad: What did you learn in school today, son?
Son: I learned that those sums you did for me were wrong.

Why are vampires so skinny?
Because they eat necks to nothing.

Why did the polite dragon keep burning his fingers?
Every time he coughed he covered his mouth.

Who are some of the werewolves' cousins?
The whatwolves and the whenwolves.

How do vampire footballers get the mud off?
They all get in the bat tub.

What's a vampire's favourite dance?
The fang-dango.

Why did the vampire stay up so late?
He had to study for his blood test.

What is the vampire's favourite slogan?
'Please Give Blood Generously'

Where does Dracula buy his pencils?
Pencil-vania.

Why did the monster go into hospital?
To have his ghoul-stones removed.

What did the lovesick Cyclops say to his sweetheart?
You're the one-eye adore.

Why did the monster cut the top of his head off?
He wanted to keep an open mind.

Why did the monster give up boxing?
He didn't want to spoil his looks.

Who is the smartest monster?
Frank-Einstein.

What did Frankenstein's monster say when he got struck by lightning?
'I needed that.'

What do you get if you cross a fashion designer
with a Scottish mystery?
The Loch Dress Monster.

Why did the Cyclops apply for half a television
licence?
Because he only had one eye.

How do you make a stupid monster think he's a
duck?
Tell him he's a duck.

What happens when you talk to a stupid monster?
Your words go in one ear and out the other three.

Why did the vampire stick a stake through his
chest?
Because he was a man after his own heart.

How can you tell when a vampire has been in a bakery?
All the jam has been sucked out of the doughnuts.

Where do monsters go for a family reunion?
Austrollia.

What do you do with a green werewolf?
Squeeze him to see if he's ripe.

What did the ghost say when he was late for work?
'If only I could get a head.'

What did the monster do when he hurt his feet?
He called a toe-truck.

How did the yeti feel when he had flu?
Abominable.

Why did the monster stop playing with his brother?
He got tired of kicking him around.

What do monsters play?
Swallow my leader.

When Dracula sent his servant out to fetch a
newspaper, why didn't he come back?
He was out for the Count.

What jewels do zombies wear?
Tombstones.

Why did the vampire take up acting?
It was in his blood.

How do vampires keep their breath smelling nice?
They use extractor fangs.

First vampire: I live on garlic alone.
Second vampire: Anyone who does that should live alone.

How do you join a vampire fan club?
Send your name, address and blood group.

Where do vampire comedians get their jokes from?
A crypt writer.

How do you find a monster on the Internet?
Use a Lurch engine.

Did you hear about the vampire that was seen crawling through the desert crying 'Blood, blood'?

First monster: I'm so thirsty my tongue's hanging out.
Second monster: Oh, I thought that was your necktie.

What did they say about the aristocratic monster?
That he was born with a silver shovel in his mouth.

What do monsters make with cars?
Traffic Jam.

How do you talk to a monster?
Use big words.

What do vampires write on their Christmas cards?
'Best vicious of the season'

What do vampires think of blood transfusions?
New-fang-led nonsense.

What does a monster mother say to her children at dinnertime?
'Don't talk with someone in your mouth.'

Why couldn't the stupid monster write the number eleven?
He didn't know which number came first.

Two stupid monsters were walking down the road and the first monster said, 'Look at that dog with one eye.' The other monster covered one of his eyes and asked, 'Where?'

First monster: What's your new boyfriend like?
Second monster: He's mean, nasty, ugly, smelly and totally evil, but he has some bad points, too.

Why didn't the monster use toothpaste?
Because he said his teeth weren't loose.

A monster and a zombie went into a funeral home.
'I'd like to order a coffin for a friend of mine who
has just died,' said the monster.
'Certainly, sir,' said the undertaker, 'but you didn't
have to bring him with you.'

Why can't Dracula write poetry?
He goes from bat to verse.

First monster: Am I late for dinner?
Second monster: Yes, everyone's been eaten.

Why did the stupid monster get so excited after he finished his jigsaw puzzle in only six months?
Because on the box it said 'From 2–4 years'.

What do vampires sing on New Year's Eve?
Auld Fang Syne.

Why is Hollywood full of vampires?
They need someone to play the bit parts.

How does a witch make scrambled eggs?
She holds the pan and gets two friends to make the stove shake with fright.

What did one of Frankenstein's monster's ears say to the other?
'I didn't know we lived on the same block.'

A skeleton walks into a bar and says to the bartender, 'I'd like a beer and a mop.'

What is large, yellow, lives in Scotland and has never been seen?
The Loch Ness Canary.

What will a monster eat in a restaurant?
The waiter.

What did the vampire say when he saw the neck of the sleeping man?
'Breakfast in bed.'

First monster: I don't think much of your sister.
Second monster: Never mind – eat the vegetables instead.

Monster: Fill me up.
Petrol pump attendant: You have to have a car for me to do that.
Monster: I had one for lunch.

First zombie: You don't look too well today.
Second zombie: No, I'm dead on my feet.

Why do vampires drink blood?
They can't afford champagne.

What do yetis drink on top of Everest?
High tea.

How did the monster cure his sore throat?
He spent all day gargoyling.

Where did the vampire bite the clown?
In his juggler vein.

First zombie: I'm sick of scaring people. It doesn't work any more.
Second zombie: Yes. We may as well be alive for all they care.

Did you hear about the comedian who entertained
at a werewolf's party?
He had them howling in the aisles.

How did the stupid monster burn his nose?
Bobbing for French fries.

When do vampires bite you?
On wincedays.

What did Dracula say to his apprentice?
'We need some new blood around here.'

What is a vampire's favourite type of boat?
A blood vessel.

First monster: Stand still. There's something ugly on your shoulder.
Second monster: Help. What is it?
First monster: Your head.

First werewolf: Nerg.
Second werewolf: Nerg, nerg, gug.
First werewolf: Don't change the subject.

Did you hear about the stupid monster who took his dog to obedience school?
The dog passed and the monster failed.

Why are stupid monsters hurt by people's words?
Because people keep hitting them with dictionaries.

What do a stupid monster and a beer bottle have in common?
They're both empty from the neck up.

What did the monster say to the grand piano?
'Darling, you've got lovely teeth.'

Where did vampires go to first in North America?
New-fang-land.

How can you tell if a stupid monster has been using the computer?
There's correction fluid on the screen.

How can you tell if another stupid monster has been using the computer?
There's writing on the correction fluid.

Why are dragons unhealthy?
Because they can't give up smoking.

Why did the stupid monster spend two weeks in a
revolving door?
Because he was looking for the doorknob.

How can you tell if a ghost is about to faint?
He goes pale as a sheet.

Did you hear about the stupid monster who went
outside with only one glove on?
The weather forecast said that it might be warm,
but on the other hand it might be quite cool.

How did the stupid monster pierce his ear?
Answering the stapler.

Did you hear about the monster who couldn't sleep
at night because he thought there were humans
under his bed?

Why aren't yetis found?
They're so big they're hardly ever lost.

Where does the bride of Frankenstein have her
hair done?
At the ugly parlour.

Which is the unluckiest monster in the world?
The Luck Less Monster.

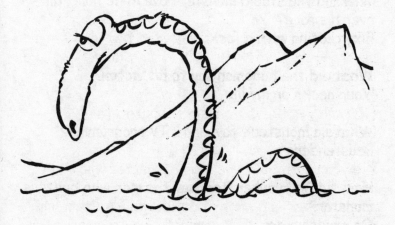

Why did the stupid monster have little holes all over his face?
From eating with a fork.

What did the hangman say to his victim?
'Your neck's on my list.'

What's a monster's favourite TV programme?
Beastenders.

How did Dr Frankenstein pay the men who built his monster?
On a piece rate.

Did you hear about the girl monster who wasn't pretty and wasn't ugly?
She was pretty ugly.

Who did the vampire fall in love with?
The girl necks door.

Did you hear about the monster who thought he was a card player?
He shuffled as he walked.

First zombie: Do you still hold your girlfriend's hand?
Second zombie: Yes, but I wish the rest of her would visit more often.

Did you hear about the stupid monster who had his address tattooed on his forehead?
That way, when he got lost he could mail himself home.

Why wouldn't the vampire eat his soup?
It clotted.

Why do stupid monsters have 'TGIF' on their shoes?
'Toes go in first'

Why did the Abominable Snowman send his father to Siberia?
Because he wanted frozen pop.

What do young female monsters do at parties?
They go around looking for edible bachelors.

Why was the dragon kicked off the newsgroup?
He kept flaming everyone.

Did you hear about the monster who is so ugly that
when a wasp stings him it shuts its eyes?

First vampire: How's life?
Second vampire: Terrible. Today I got a letter
saying I'm overdrawn by fifty pints at the blood
bank.

Why did the stupid monster put his hands over his
ears?
He was trying to hold on to a thought.

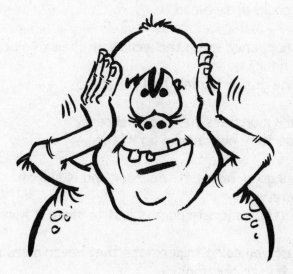

Why did the vampire buy a red pen?
So he could draw blood.

What happened when the werewolf chewed a bone
for an hour?
When he got up he only had three legs.

Why are monsters such bad dancers?
Because they have seven left feet.

What is grey, howls at the moon and is full of
concrete?
A wolf (the concrete part is just to make it harder).

What do you call a triceratops that never gives up?
A try, try, triceratops.

What did the zombie's friend say when he introduced him to his girlfriend?
'Good grief. Where did you dig her up from?'

Did you hear about the monster who had an extra pair of hands?
He kept them in a handbag.

Why did the monster bring toilet paper to the birthday party?
Because he was a party pooper.

What did the monster do after he had his teeth pulled out?
He ate the dentist.

What monster sits on the end of your finger?
The bogeyman.

Why was the werewolf arrested in the butcher's shop?
He was chop lifting.

What keeps zombies cheerful?
Knowing that every shroud has a silver lining.

Why did the small werewolf bite the girl's ankle?
Because he couldn't reach any higher.

What happened when King Kong swallowed Big Ben?
He found it time-consuming.

First monster: I have a hunch.
Second monster: I thought you were a funny shape.

What do you get when you offer a stupid monster a penny for his thoughts?
Change.

Where do American vampires work?
In the Vampire State Building.

Why do they have a fence around the graveyard?
Everyone is dying to get in.

First monster: My, hasn't your little girl grown?
Second monster: Yes, she's certainly gruesome.

What does a tired vampire do?
He takes a coffin break.

Did you hear about the stupid monster who had
'left' and 'right' tattooed on his toes so he would
know which feet his shoes should go on? Trouble
was, he couldn't read.

Did you hear about the stupid monster who lost his
shoes because he put them on the wrong feet?
He couldn't remember whose feet he put them on.

What did Dracula say to the Wolf man?
'You look like you're going to the dogs.'

What happened when the werewolf swallowed a clock?
He got ticks.

What kind of fur do you get from a werewolf?
As fur away as you can.

What does a stupid monster say if you blow in his ear?
'Thanks for the refill.'

What's fat, purple and wobbles?
A fat, purple jelly monster.

What do you call a monster's index finger?
His handkerchief.

What has eight legs and can't hold a tune?
Four tone-deaf monsters carol singing.

Why was the vampire thought of as simple-minded?
Because he was a complete sucker.

Why did the monster put bird seed in his shoes?
Because he had pigeon toes.

What do you call a ten foot monster?
Shorty.

Do monsters snore?
Only when they're asleep.

What type of people do vampires like?
O positive people.

Why was the young vampire a failure?
Because he fainted at the sight of blood.

A monster went outside in the rain but not a hair on
his head got wet. How come?
He didn't have a head.

I used to be a werewolf but I'm all right
noooooooowwwwww . . .

Why did the sea monster eat five ships that were
carrying potatoes?
Nobody can eat just one potato ship.

What cereal does Dracula eat for breakfast?
Ready-neck.

How do you make a monster's eyes light up?
Shine a torch in his ear.

What do you see when you look into a stupid
monster's eyes?
The back of his head.

Did you hear about the monster who plugged his electric blanket into the toaster by mistake?
He spent the night popping in and out of bed.

How can you tell a troll would be a good gardener?
They all have green thumbs.

Why did the monster lie on his back?
To trip up low-flying aircraft.

Why did the monster stop wearing a flower in his buttonhole?
The pot kept hitting him in the chest.

Why did the monster get a ticket?
He ran through a stomp sign.

How does a stupid monster know if he's on his way home or on his way to work?
He opens his lunch box to see if there is anything inside.

How many stupid monsters does it take to make chocolate-chip cookies?
Ten. One to mix the dough and nine to peel the Smarties.

How do you drown a stupid monster?
Put a scratch 'n' sniff sticker at the bottom of a swimming pool.

What do you do when a stupid monster throws a hand grenade at you?
Pull the pin and throw it back.

What do you do when a stupid monster throws a pin at you?
Run. He's got a hand grenade in his mouth.

What is a vampire's favourite kind of coffee?
De-coffin-ated.

Where do ghosts live?
In dead ends.

Did you hear about the monster who had twelve arms and no legs?
He was all fingers and thumbs.

Why did the stupid monster put his finger over the nail when he was hammering?
The noise gave him a headache.

How does a vampire clean his house?
With a victim cleaner.

Why couldn't the stupid monster make ice cubes?
He lost the recipe.

How does an alien count to 23?
On its fingers.

Teacher: What is half of eight?
Jamie: Up and down, or across?
Teacher: What do you mean?
Jamie: Well Sir, up and down it's 0, and across it's 3.

What animal is best at maths?
Rabbits – they multiply fastest.

Did you know that 5/4 people are bad with fractions?

Which sea creature is good at maths?
An octoplus.

Why are mathematicians good at dancing?
Because they've got logarithms.

Why shouldn't you mention the number 288 in polite company?
It's just two gross.

What does everyone have that they can always count on?
Fingers.

How do toads count to fifty?
On their warts.

Did you hear about the mathematical plants?
They grew square roots.

What's the longest piece of furniture in the world?
A multiplication table.

What makes long division hard work?
All those numerals you have to carry.

If you add 20,567 to 23,678 and then divide by 97
what do you get?
The wrong answer.

If two's company and three's a crowd, what are four
and five?
Nine.

How do you count cows?
With a cow-culator.

How many people are buried in that cemetery?
All of them.

What is 5Q + 5Q?
10Q
You're welcome.

Where do police officers live?
999 Letsby Avenue.

What is Santa's phone number?
0,0,0

If there are 99 people in a boat and it flips over,
how many people will there be?
66.

What did the zero say to the eight?
'Nice belt.'

What do you do if the M6 is closed?
Drive up the M3 twice.

What lies on the forest floor, a hundred feet up in the air?
A dead centipede.

Aren't you going to your friend's birthday party?
No. The invitation said 'from four to six' and I'm seven.

What goes up but doesn't come down?
Your age.

What do you call two tutus?
A four four.

NUTTY
NAMES

What do you call sticky coffee?
Toffee.

What do you call sticky coffee with milk?
Tofu.

What do you call an old volcano?
A blast from the past.

What do you call a man who catches bluebottles
with a fishing rod?
A fly fisherman.

What do you call a dog that sneezes a lot?
A Choowawa.

What do you call a pig with three eyes?
A piiig.

What do you call the end of a biscuit?
A bourbon conclusion.

What do you call a person who steals pigs?
A hamburglar.

What do you call an elephant that's small and pink?
A failure.

What do you call a tree that fits on your hand?
A palm.

What do you call a yeti in a phone box?
Stuck.

What do you call someone who is afraid of Santa Claus?
Claustrophobic.

What do you call a bike that keeps biting people?
A vicious cycle.

What do you call a woodpecker with no beak?
A headbanger.

What do you call a rich frog?
A gold-blooded reptile.

What do you call a monkey on top of a cake?
A marzipanzee.

What do you call an elephant that mutters?
A mumbo jumbo.

What do you call a Scottish parrot?
A Macaw.

What do you call a large person who keeps ringing
people and pretending to be someone else?
A big phone-y.

What do you call a pickle that draws?
A dillustrator.

What do you call an anaesthesiologist who shows up for work wearing a rabbit suit?
The Ether Bunny.

What do you call a chicken in a shell suit?
An egg.

What do you call a pig in a butcher's shop?
A pork chop.

What do you call a watch in the 25th century?
Future-wrist-tic.

What do you call a surgeon with eight arms?
A doctopus.

What do you call a spider that gambles?
A big spinder.

What do you call small Indian guitars?
Baby sitars.

What do you call a bee born in May?
A maybe.

What do you call cows with a sense of humour?
Laughing stock.

What do you call an overweight alien?
An extra-cholesterol.

What do you call a flying skunk?
A smellicopter.

What do you call little piles of rubbish?
Dumplings.

What do you call five bottles of lemonade?
A pop group.

What do you call a girl who lives between two houses?
Elaine.

What do you call mad sea cow disease?
Manatee insanity.

What do you call well-behaved fog?
Conformist.

What do you call friends on a ship?
Friendships.

What's the name of the little girl who went out
saving wolves?
Little Green Riding Hood.

What do you call an egg that won't co-operate?
An impractical yoke.

What do you call a judge with no thumbs?
Justice Fingers.

What do you call an elephant disguised as a nun?
A creature of habit.

What do you call a parrot that's coming apart?
A paraphrase.

What do you call a crowd of panicking snakes?
Mass hissteria.

What do you call a sick chemist?
Indispensable.

What do you call a flag in a toilet?
Bog-standard.

What do you call it when vampires play cricket for five days?
A blood test.

What do you call a concrete path leading to a diving board?
A dive-way.

What do you call a bank in the Arctic?
A slush fund.

What do you call a juicy ant?
An anteloupe.

What do you call an ejector seat on a helicopter?
A bad idea.

What do you call a thick vampire?
A stupid clot.

What's it called when you borrow money to buy a bison?
A buffaloan.

What do you call a goblin with a twisted ankle?
A hoblin goblin.

What do you call a rotten hot dog?
A rankfurter.

What do you call a hippy's wife?
Mississippi.

What do you call a boxer wearing pigskin gloves?
Ham-fisted.

What do you call zombies in a belfry?
Dead ringers.

What do you call a rich melon?
A melon-aire.

What do you call a frog with no hind legs?
Unhoppy.

What do you call an Ancient Egyptian ruler with no teeth?
A gummy mummy.

What do you call a boy mermaid?
A merdude.

What do you call a ghost who only haunts the town hall?
The nightmayor.

What do you call a dance for people who hate each other?
An avoidance.

What's the rear entrance to a cafeteria called?
The bacteria.

What is a buttress?
A female goat.

What do you call a person who can't weave?
Unbeweaveable.

What do you call a goose who likes eating prunes?
A loose goose.

What do you call a traffic warden who never fines anyone?
A triffic warden.

What do you call a rhino who drinks too much?
A whino.

What do you call a baby turkey?
A goblet.

What do you call it when you lease false teeth?
A dental rental.

What do you call a neurotic octopus?
A crazy, mixed-up squid.

Did you hear about the little boy who was named
after his father?
They called him Dad.

What do you call ten hairdressers standing in a
line?
A barberqueue.

What do you call a rabbit on a diet?
Thinning hare.

What do you call a man who claps at Christmas?
Santapplause.

What do you call the ghost who haunts TV shows?
Phantom of the Oprah.

What do you call a secret agent who hides in the bushes?
James Frond.

What do you call a blonde police officer?
A fair cop.

What do you call an American drawing?
A Yankee Doodle.

What do you call ant space travellers?
Cosmonants.

What should you call a bald teddy?
Fred bear.

What do you call a cat with no legs?
Dogfood.

What do you call a girl with a rabbit trap on her knee?
Courtney.

What do you call an alien with no eyes?
Alan.

What do you call roller bladers who surf the Net?
Online skaters.

What do you call a goat that is a professional comedian?
Billy the Kid.

What do you call a running chicken?
Poultry in motion.

What do you call an ant that likes to be alone?
An independant.

What's it called when you ignore a bad toilet?
Evil-loo-shun.

What do you call a vicar on a motorbike?
Rev.

What do you call a woman with a pint of beer on her head playing snooker?
Beatrix Potter.

What do you call a snake that is trying to become a bird?
A feather boa.

What do you call a woman who hangs from the chandelier?
Crystal.

What do you call a goat that lives on a mountain?
A hillbilly.

What do you call a baby foot soldier?
Infantry.

What do you call a mammoth that conducts an orchestra?
Tuskanini.

What do you call a nervous celery stalk?
An edgy veggie.

What do you call a vampire after it is one year old?
A two-year-old vampire.

What do you call a game of football where both
teams are angels?
A match made in heaven.

What do you call a fake noodle?
Impasta.

What do you call a pig that took a plane?
Swine flu.

What's the dumbest fish in the school called?
Dinner.

What do you call a teacher who makes fireworks?
A headbanger.

What do you call a convertible donkey?
A sofa-Ned.

What do you call a puzzle at the top of a pyramid?
A cone-under-'em.

What do you call a big cat with curling tongues?
A corrugated lion.

What do you call a dream where you're being
attacked by vampires?
A bitemare.

What is a hairdresser's licence called?
A perm-it.

What do you call a ghost's mother and father?
Transparents.

What do you call a fat skeleton?
A failure.

What would we be called if everyone lived in their cars?
An in-car-nation.

What do you call A Tale of Two Mosquitoes?
A bite-time story.

What do you call a special agent in a washing-up bottle?
Bubble O 7.

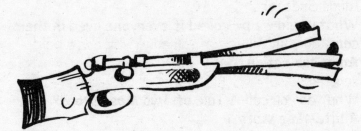

What do you call a rifle with three barrels?
A trifle.

What do you call the small rivers that run into the
Nile?
The juve-Niles.

What do you call a skeleton who goes out in the
snow and rain without a coat or an umbrella?
A numbskull.

What do you call a dog that studies the bones it
digs up?
A Barkyologist.

What do you call it when an aeroplane disappears
over the horizon?
Boeing, going, gone.

What do you call a Roman emperor with flu?
Julius Sneezer.

What do you call lice on someone who has a bald
head?
Homeless.

What does a dentist call his X-rays?
Tooth-pics.

What do you call a small stupid hill?
A pillock.

What do you call a drunken ghost?
A methylated spirit.

What do you call a piece of wood that has nothing to do?
Board.

What do you call a highly-skilled plumber?
A drain surgeon.

What do you call a nun with a washing machine on her head?
Sister-Matic.

What do you call the spot in the middle of a graveyard?
The dead centre.

What do you call a cow with two legs?
Lean beef.

What do you call a gorilla that works as a car mechanic?
A grease monkey.

What do you call a lonely, love-sick statue?
Art broken.

What do you call a monkey holding a bomb?
A baboom.

What do you call a hairy monster in a river?
A weir-wolf.

What do you call the history of a car?
An autobiography.

What do you call a cannibal who eats his mother's sister?
An aunt-eater.

What do you call the man who went to a fancy dress party as a sandwich?
Roland Butter.

What do you call a Spaniard who can't find his car?
Carlos.

What do you call twin vampires?
Blood brothers.

What do you call a man with a swarm of bees round his head?
A. B. Hive.

What do you call a train with bubble gum on it?
A chew chew train.

What do you call Australian boxer shorts?
Down underwear.

What do you call a Viking with a sore throat?
A Norse Whisperer.

What do you call two men sitting above a window sill?
Curt and Rod.

What do you call a cow spying on another cow?
A steak out.

What do you call a fruit that stays up very late to study for tests?
A cramberry.

What do you call a peeled potato?
A spuddy in the nuddy.

What do you call a perforated relic?
A holey grail.

What do you call a pelican that can't do anything?
A pelican't.

What do John the Baptist and Winnie the Pooh have in common?
They have the same middle name.

What do you call a flock of birds flying in formation?
The red sparrows.

What do you call a whale that can't stop talking?
A blubber mouth.

What do you call a really stupid ballet dance?
A pas de d'oh.

What do you call a fish with no eyes?
A fsh.

What do you call a sick dog?
A germy shepherd.

What do you call a lemon with a zipper on it?
A fruit fly.

What do you call a man who inherits a dairy?
A dairy heir.

What do you call a woman who is crunchy and thin?
Crisp-tine.

What do you call an Italian with a rubber toe?
Roberto.

What do you call a musical instrument that is played
by two teams of twenty people?
A piano forty.

What do you call a hippopotamus without a tail?
A hippobottomless.

What do you call a stolen yam?
A hot potato.

What do you call a rabbit dressed up as a cake?
A cream bun.

What do you call a man whose father was a canon?
A son of a gun.

What do you call a female worm?
A worman.

What do you call a pig that plays football?
A ball hog.

What do you call a pen with no hair?
A bald point.

What do you call a dog in jeans and a sweater?
A plain clothes police dog.

What do you call a dog in the middle of a muddy path?
A mutt in a rut.

What do you call a clever duck?
A wise quacker.

What do you call a scared biscuit?
A cowardy custard cream.

What do you call a hearing aid made from fruit?
A lemonade.

What do you call a woman who eats shells?
Conchita.

What do you call a frozen cat?
A catsicle.

What do you call a sleepwalking nun?
A roaming Catholic.

What do you call two banana peels?
A pair of slippers.

What do you call an Igloo without a toilet?
An Ig.

What do you call a flying turtle?
A shellicopter.

What do you call the ice cream truck man?
A sundae driver.

PATHETIC
PUNS

Why should you never insult an alien?
You might hurt its feelers.

What does a wizard say to improve his sight?
'Hocus focus.'

Did you hear about the pregnant bedbug?
She had her baby in the spring.

Why did the termite eat a sofa and two chairs?
It had a suite tooth.

What did one tooth say to the other?
'Get your cap on, the dentist is taking us out
tonight.'

Why does a chicken coop have only two doors?
If it had four, it would be a chicken sedan.

What dance does a tin-opener do?
The Can-Can.

What should you do if a bull charges you?
Pay up.

What is the cheapest way to get to Iceland?
Be born there.

When can't astronauts visit the moon?
When it's full.

What is a specimen?
An Italian astronaut.

What did the Martian say when he landed in a flower bed?
'Take me to your weeder.'

Why did the witch stand up in front of an audience?
She had to give a screech.

Why do aliens keep flying past Peter Pan's house?
They see a sign that says 'Never Never Land'.

Pilot: Mayday. Starboard engine on fire.
Control tower: State your height and position.
Pilot: I'm five foot seven and I'm sitting in the cockpit.

What did the musical alien say?
'Take me to your leider.'

Why was the ground greasy?
Because the rain was dripping.

How do you avoid falling hair?
Jump out of the way.

How do you help a donkey?
Give assistance.

What should you do if you feel nauseous in church?
Look for the box by the door that says 'For the Sick'.

Why is lightning badly behaved?
It doesn't know how to conduct itself.

Who is the smallest mum in the world?
Minimum.

Did you hear about the play called A Broken Leg?
Apparently it had a strong cast.

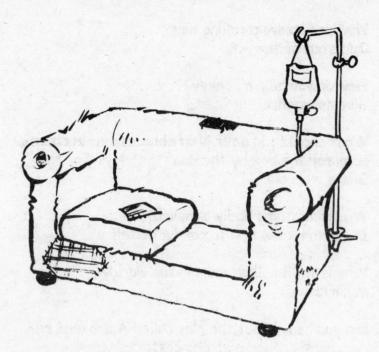

Where in a hospital can you mend an old sofa?
In the recovery room.

Why was the moth so unpopular?
He kept picking holes in everyone.

If we breathe oxygen in the daytime, what do we
breathe at night?
Nitrogen.

Why are sheep always broke?
Because they keep getting fleeced.

Who was too heavy to go to the ball?
Cinderelephant.

What's a hanky for?
Cold storage.

What's a twip?
When a wabbit falls over.

What happened to the ship which ran aground on a purple beach?
It was marooned.

What do you get if you swap a German sausage for a sea bird?
You take a tern for the wurst.

What do you give a train driver for Christmas?
Platform shoes.

What does a French person eat at eight o'clock in the morning?
Huit-heure-bix.

Why are cornfields crowded?
The corn stands ear to ear.

Where's spaghetti junction?
Just pasta Birmingham.

What do you tell a chicken that won't leave you alone?
'Just peck it in.'

What did the wasp say to the fly?
'I must fly now but I'll give you a buzz later.'

What did the lettuce say when it was squeezed?
'Lettuce go.'

How did the sunbathing frog die?
Heat croak.

What did the big hand say to the little hand?
'I'll be back in an hour.'

How do you cure a shy pebble?
Make it a little boulder.

Policeman: I'm looking for a man with a hearing aid.
Policewoman: Wouldn't a pair of binoculars be more useful?

What's a character line?
What your mum calls her wrinkles.

What's a dog's favourite musical?
The Hound of Music.

What did one lift say to the other lift?
'I think I'm going down with something.'

What do moths study in school?
Mothematics.

How much is an American skunk worth?
One scent.

How do pigs make coffee?
With a coffee porkulator.

Why are geese bad drivers?
They honk all the time.

Why did the reporter walk into the ice cream shop?
Because he wanted a scoop.

Why are adult deer expensive?
Because they're big bucks.

Why is a pancake like a cricket team?
Because they both need a good batter.

Why are barbers such good drivers?
Because they know all the shortcuts.

What's the definition of an arms race?
An octopus running for a bus.

Why was the glow-worm confused?
It didn't know whether it was coming or glowing.

What card do you bow down to?
The master card.

Why is a sloppy waiter like an entrepreneur?
Because they both have a finger in many pies.

How do horses propose?
They go down on bended neigh.

Have you heard about the amazing new discovery?
It's a pill that is half aspirin and half glue for people
who have splitting headaches.

Why did the mother cat put stamps on all her
kittens?
She wanted to post a litter.

What does a dinosaur say when he wants to leave
the dinner table?
'May I be extinct please?'

What kind of trees do plumbers plant?
Toiletries.

What did the volcano have at the party?
A blast.

'Good morning, Judge, how do you feel?'
'Fine, £100!'

Where do lions get their clothes?
Jungle sales.

What's pink and fluffy?
Pink fluff.

Why was the ant practising golf in the saucer?
Because he was playing golf in the cup the next day.

Why did the apple cry?
Its peelings were hurt.

What happened to the butcher who sat on his bacon slicer?
He got a little behind with his work.

Two vultures on an aeroplane, each carrying two dead racoons. The stewardess stops them and says, 'I'm sorry, only one carrion allowed per passenger.'

What happens if you keep your nose to the grindstone?
You get a flat face.

'How's your job as a cocktail barman going?'
'Oh, it's no great shakes.'

What do cavemen eat at picnics?
Club sandwiches.

What is the best way to prevent wrinkles?
Don't sleep in your clothes.

What did the can say to the can opener?
'You make me flip my lid.'

How did the clairvoyant know what his brother was
getting for Christmas?
He felt his presents.

How do you learn to be a litter collector?
You just pick it up as you go along.

Tom: My sister fell down a flight of stairs.
Sophie: Cellar?
Tom: No, I think she can be repaired.

Why did the king go to the dentist?
To get his teeth crowned.

What's the smallest animal in the jungle?
A shrimpanzee.

Why did the homeless man fall off the toilet?
Because he had no fixed commode.

What do iron chickens do?
They come home to rust.

Did you hear about the robber who got arrested for flat feet?
His feet were in the wrong flat.

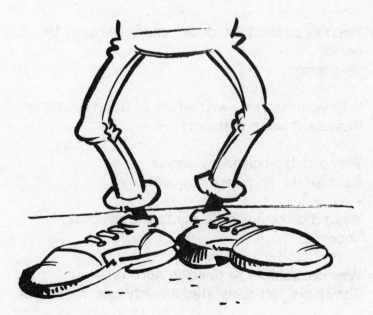

What's red and blue, drunk, and flies round the world?
Stuporman.

Why was the story writing competition a disaster?
Because it was a write-off.

Why was the calendar worried?
Because its days were numbered.

What did the boy book say to the girl book?
'Page me.'

Why are solders so tired on April 1st?
They have just completed a thirty-one day March.

What do you find up a clean nose?
Fingerprints.

Why was the mother flea sad?
All her children went to the dogs.

How do your teeth stay together?
With toothpaste.

Why did the man hit the fortune teller when she started laughing?
He was striking a happy medium.

Where can you learn to make ice cream?
In sundae school.

What kind of motorbike can cook eggs?
A scrambler.

What's an equator?
Something that eats quators.

Why are cats longer in the evening than they are in the morning?
Because they're let out in the evening and taken in in the morning.

Why is butter dishonest?
Because it always greases your palm.

Is that seat saved?
No, but we're still praying for it.

What alien has the best hearing?
The eeriest.

Why did the businessman take a deer on Concorde?
He wanted to make a fast buck.

What did the Martian say to the gas pump?
'Take your finger out of your ear when I'm talking
to you.'

How does the man in the moon cut his hair?
Eclipse it.

If Q is having a tea party and all the other letters
of the alphabet were invited, which would be late?
U,V,X,Y and Z because they all come after tea.

Why did the plumber lose everything?
His job went down the drain.

What happened to the man who couldn't keep up payments to his exorcist?
He was repossessed.

Why is money called dough?
Because we all knead it.

What's stupid and chilly?
A thick cold.

How did the mother buffalo say farewell to her son?
'Bison.'

What does a house wear?
Address.

Did you hear about the fire at the circus?
The flames were in tents.

How does a mummy begin a letter?
'Tomb it may concern . . .'

Why was the belt sent to jail?
For holding up a pair of trousers.

Why did the sword swallower only swallow half a sword?
He was having a mid-knife crisis.

What did the Shakespearian cat say?
'Ta-bby or not ta-bby.'

Why are cows always broke?
The farmers milk them dry.

Where are teachers made?
On an assembly line.

Why did the fish have such a big phone bill?
Because once it got on the line it couldn't get off.

What did one test dummy ask another?
'Can I crash at your place tonight?'

How do undertakers speak?
Gravely.

What did the Buddhist say to the hot dog vendor?
'Make me one with everything.'

What does a vegetarian earn?
A celery.

Who is the heaviest fairy story character?
Little Lead Riding Hood.

Where did the kittens go on a class trip?
To the meow-seum.

Why is it hard to bury an elephant?
Because it's a huge undertaking.

What do you say when a dog runs away?
'Dog-gone.'

Why are rocks ungrateful?
They take everything for granite.

Why did the ambitious lad quit his job in the chip shop?
He had bigger fish to fry.

Why did the man chain his granny to a sea lion?
Because he was trying to keep biddy and seal together.

Why did the poker player hug William Shakespeare?
Because he always held his bards close to his chest.

Why can't you make a million pounds laugh?
Because it's serious money.

Why did the clown cross the road?
To find his rubber chicken.

Why do mice fall over when you cut them in half?
Because a mouse divided against itself cannot stand.

What's more dangerous than being with a fool?
Fooling with a bee.

Where do fish keep their money?
In an off-shore account.

What did one volcano say to the other volcano?
'Do you larva me like I larva you?'

What did the fireman's wife get for Christmas?
A ladder in her stocking.

What is a baby's motto?
'If at first you don't succeed cry, cry again.'

What did the banana say when the judge asked him
what he was doing?
'I'm appealing my case.'

A policewoman spots a man driving and knitting at
the same time. Pulling up beside him, she shouts out
of the window, 'Pull over.'
'No,' he shouts back, 'a pair of socks!'

Which American state do babies drink milk from?
Califormula.

How do you know Rapunzel liked to go to parties?
She liked to let her hair down.

Why does toothpaste always fail?
Because it goes down the tubes.

How could the girl tell that her clock was hungry?
Because it went back four seconds.

A man breaks down on the motorway. Another motorist stops and asks, 'Would you like a hand?' The man replies, 'No thanks, I'm waiting for a toe.'

What happened to the useless woodcutter?
He was axed.

How do we know that the Earth won't come to an end?
Because it's round.

Who is the biggest gangster in the sea?
Al Caprawn.

What do you put in a www.ashing machine?
Net curtains.

How do really small people call each other?
With microphones.

What did one cloud say to the other?
'I'm cirrus about you.'

Why doesn't the sea spill over the earth?
Because it's tide.

What made the Tower of Pisa lean?
It stopped eating its pasta.

Did you hear about the vicar who turned up at the wrong funeral?
He made a grave error.

Why does the corn get mad at the farmer?
Because he is always pulling on its ears.

How do two pieces of string talk to each other?
They use twine language.

A woman entered ten different puns in a pun contest, hoping that at least one of them would win. Unfortunately, no pun in ten did.

Why did the moth nibble a hole in the carpet?
He wanted to see the floor show.

Why did the candles fall in love?
They met their match.

What did the undertaker say to his girlfriend?
'Em-balmy about you.'

Why did the cowboy pitch his tent on top of the stove?
Because he wanted a home on the range.

Did you hear about the paper company that folded?

What did one toe say to the other toe?
'Don't look now, but there's a heel following us.'

What do you call a snobbish prisoner walking down the stairs?
A condescending con descending.

What is a roll call?
The noise made by a sesame bun.

What is a flood?
A river that's too big for its bridges.

What does a pickle say when he wants to play cards?
'Dill me in.'

What's green and slimy and goes 'hith'?
A snake with a lisp.

What kind of teeth do you get for a dollar?
Buck teeth.

Why did the scarecrow win an award?
He was outstanding in his field.

What's frozen water?
Ice.
What's frozen cream?
Ice cream.
What's frozen tea?
Iced tea.
What's frozen ink?
Iced ink.
Go and take a bath then.

What do you call a snake that is trying to become a bird?
A feather boa.

Sign in a cafe: 'All drinking water in this establishment has been personally passed by the management.'

What part of the body is like a sandwich meat?
Below-knee.

Why did the balloon factory close down?
It couldn't keep up with inflation.

What colour are the sun and the wind?
The sun rose and the wind blew.

How's work at the garden centre?
Things keep cropping up.

What is a reptile's favourite dance?
Snake, rattle and roll.

Whose parrot said, 'Pieces of four, pieces of four'?
Short John Silver.

What is deceit?
Da back of your trousers.

What did the executioner say to his wife?
'Only thirty chopping days to Christmas.'

What did the snake say to the cornered rat?
'Hiss is the end of the line, buddy.'

What did one snake say when the other snake asked him the time?
'Don't asp me.'

What did Neptune say when the sea dried up?
'I haven't a notion.'

Why did the banana inspector get the sack?
He kept slipping up.

Do undertakers enjoy their job?
Of corpse they do!

What is the definition of sunburn?
Getting what you basked for.

How do you become a professor?
By degrees.

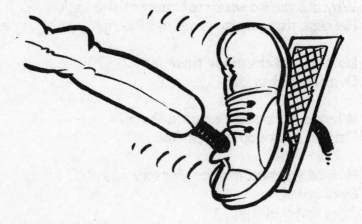

How do you top a car?
Tep on the brake, tupid.

What jungle animal shouldn't get wet?
A rhinocerust.

What did the electrician say when his son arrived
home from school late?
'Wire you insulate?'

Did you hear about the man who bought a paper
shop?
It blew away.

How do you start a jelly race?
'Get set . . .'

Where do the Chinese make car horns?
Hong King.

Why is Russia a very fast country?
Because the people are always Russian.

How do fish dry their fins?
In a fin dryer.

Why was the ghost arrested?
He didn't have a haunting licence.

What happened to the two red blood cells when
they fell in love?
They loved in vein.

Woman: Officer, you must help. I've lost my wig.
Police officer: We'll comb the area.

Why are doctors like boxers?
Because they are always jabbing people.

Which country has no fat people?
Finland.

This autumn my granny knitted me three socks for
my birthday.
Why?
Because I phoned her to say I had grown a foot
during the summer.

What did the teddy bear say when he was offered
dessert?
'No thanks, I'm stuffed.'

Did you hear about the man who was sent to prison
for something he didn't do?
He didn't jump into the getaway car fast enough.

What parts of a donkey are the oldest?
Donkey's ears.

Which musical instrument can you use to catch
fish?
Castanet.

How do locomotives hear?
Through their engineers.

What happened to the thief who stole some corn?
He got three ears.

Why did the clock go to the doctor?
It was run down.

Why was the murderer hanged in the evening?
Because it was the six o'clock noose.

How long does it take to burn a candle down?
About a wick.

What happened to the boy who swallowed a torch?
He hiccuped with delight.

How do elephants clean their clothes?
In a squashing machine.

How do shepherds gamble?
They play the sheepsteak.

What's the funniest state in America?
Joke-lahoma.

What did Hamlet say when he went camping and lost his tent.
'Tepee or not tepee, that is the question.'

Why did the unemployed fire fighter go to the plastic surgeon?
He wanted a hose job.

Do hamsters go on safaris?
Not safaris I know.

Did you hear about the florist who had two children?
One's a budding genius and the other's a blooming idiot.

What happened to the boat that sank in the sea full of piranha fish?
It came back with a skeleton crew.

What is a ghost-proof bicycle?
One with no spooks in it.

What type of tree gets the most diseases?
A sycamore.

Why is perfume obedient?
Because it is scent wherever it goes.

Why was the pig arrested?
He didn't have a grunting licence.

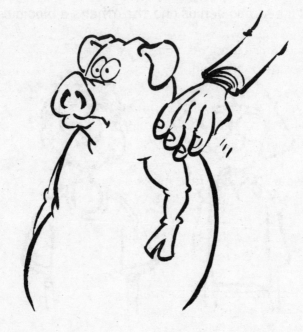

How did the glamorous ghost earn her living?
She was a cover ghoul.

Why did the villain start thinking about the old
times when he was on the gallows?
He felt noose-talgic.

Why would Snow White make a good judge?
Because she's the fairest one of all.

How does a dogcatcher get paid?
By the pound.

Why did the tree dye its hair?
Because its roots were showing.

Why did the gold prospector quit his job?
Things just didn't pan out.

Why did the bees go on strike?
Because they wanted more honey and shorter
working flowers.

How does a boat show its affection?
It hugs the shore.

How do you make a moth ball?
Flick its nose.

What calamities happen every twenty-four hours?
Day breaks and night falls.

How do you fix a short circuit?
Lengthen it.

What is hail?
Hard boiled rain.

What kind of pine has the sharpest needles?
A porcupine.

Why are tall people lazy?
Because they lie longer in bed.

What makes grass so dangerous?
The blades.

'I'll lend you a dollar if you promise not to keep it
too long.'
'Oh, I won't. I'll spend it right away.'

Why did the farmer give his little chicks ear
muffs?
So they wouldn't overhear fowl language.

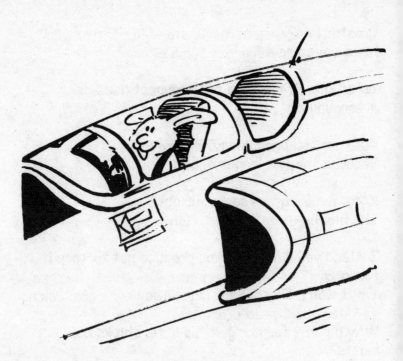

Where do rabbits learn to fly?
In the Hare Force.

What do bees chew?
Bumble gum.

What did one crisp say to the other crisp?
'Let's go for a dip.'

How did the patient get to the hospital so fast?
Flu.

What does an octopus wear when it's cold?
A coat of arms.

Why did the famous movie stars go to the river?
They wanted to give out some otter-graphs.

What do you use to cut the ocean in half?
A sea-saw.

What's yellow and brown and covered in
blackberries?
A bramble bee.

What do you call four bullfighters in quicksand?
Quatro sinko.

News flash: 'Today a cement mixer crashed into a
police van carrying prisoners. The police are looking
for some hardened criminals . . .'

Which dinosaur is the loudest at night?
A brontosnaurus.

Stuart: How did you find the weather on your
holiday?
Jenny: I just went outside and there it was.

Where does a ghost train stop?
At a manifestation.

What happens when business is slow at a medicine
factory?
You can hear a cough drop.

What do you get from a pampered cow?
Spoiled milk.

PREPOSTEROUS
PETS

Why is a puppy good at DIY?
Because it's always doing little jobs around the house.

What's a cat's favourite exercise?
Pussups.

What's a cat's favourite cake?
A catameringue.

Motorist: I'm sorry, I've just run over your cat. I'd like to replace it.
Owner: How good are you at catching mice?

Stuart: My dog's got no tail.
Jenny: How do you know if he's happy?
Stuart: He stops biting me.

Where do computers take their sick pets?
To the Intervet.

My horse is very polite. When we come to a jump, he stops and lets me go first.

Why did the old English sheepdog go to the optician?
Everything was all fuzzy.

What should you know before you teach your dog tricks?
More than the dog.

What happened when the dog went to a flea circus?
He stole the show.

Good news. I've been given a goldfish for my birthday . . . the bad news is that I don't get the bowl until my next birthday.

What do you give a dog with a fever?
Mustard – it's the best thing for a hot dog.

Stuart: That ointment the vet gave me for the dog makes my fingers smart.
Jenny: Why don't you rub some on your head then?

Sign in the window of a pet store: 'For Sale – Pedigree bulldog. House trained. Eats anything. Very fond of children.'

Which pets are always found lying around the house?
Carpets.

Why do cats cough up fur balls?
Because they love a good gag.

My dog's legs are so short, when he goes for a walk
they don't even reach the floor.

What is a dog's favourite sport?
Formula One drooling.

How is cat food sold?
Usually purr can.

Stuart: Did you change the water in the fishbowl?
Jenny: No. They didn't finish the water I gave them
yesterday.

What do cats eat for breakfast?
Mew-sli.

What kind of car does a cat drive?
A Cat-a-lac.

Did you know that the first animal in space was a dog?
Everything went fine until he stuck his head out of the window.

Stuart: Would you like to play with our new dog?
Jenny: He looks very fierce. Does he bite?
Stuart: That's what I want to find out.

Did you put the cat out?
I didn't know it was on fire.

How did the soldier put a tank in his house?
It was a fish tank.

On what should you mount a statue of your cat?
A caterpillar.

What do you call a dog that gets mail?
A golden receiver.

Why do you have to wait so long for a ghost train to come along?
They only run a skeleton service.

My parrot lays square eggs.
- That's amazing. Can it talk as well?
Yes, but only one word.
- What's that?
'Ouch.'

Our dog is a good watchdog. Yesterday he watched while someone burgled our house.

How does an idiot call for his dog?
He puts two fingers in his mouth and then shouts 'Rover'.

See my cat? He's just drunk a hundred saucers of milk.
That must be a lap record.

Did you hear about the dog who ran a hundred miles just to pick up a stick?
It was a little farfetched.

Where do cats like to go on vacation?
The Canary Islands.

Why do dogs run in circles?
Because it's hard to run in squares.

When is a black dog not a black dog?
When it's a greyhound.

First boy: My dog is so clever he can go to the butcher's and buy meat.
Second boy: I know.
First boy: How do you know?
Second boy: My cat told me.

Why do you need a licence for a dog and not for a cat?
Cats can't drive.

Did you hear about the man who went to the fancy
dress party as a bone?
A dog ate him in the hall.

Why did the poor dog chase his own tail?
He was trying to make both ends meet.

How do you know if your cat has eaten a duck?
It has that down in the mouth look.

Jenny: Do you have any cats going cheap?
Pet shop owner: No, they usually go 'Meow'.

Louisa: Mum and Dad just bought me a keet.
Tom: Don't you mean a parakeet?
Louisa: No, they only bought me one.

What looks like half a cat?
The other half.

Which cats purr more than any other?
Purrsians.

Jamie: I was the teacher's pet last year.
Jenny: Why was that?
Jamie: She couldn't afford a dog.

RAVING
RIDDLES

Which side of the moon has the most craters?
The outside.

When is homework not homework?
When it's turned into the teacher.

How do you make a net?
Sew lots of holes together.

What is the one thing everybody in the world is doing at the same time?
Growing older.

How is playing the bagpipes like throwing a javelin blindfolded?
You don't have to be good to get everyone's attention.

What can you put in a cup but not take out again?
A crack.

What's green and eats bananas?
A septic monkey.

What's big and green and has a trunk?
An unripe elephant.

What grows up and down at the same time?
A gosling.

What's white and goes up?
A snowflake with no sense of direction.

What's an inkling?
A baby fountain pen.

How can you tell the really stupid guy at the airport?
He's the one throwing bread to the aeroplanes.

What is green and fluffy?
A seasick poodle.

What's pointed in one direction and headed in the other?
A pin.

When shouldn't you trust a smiling cow?
When it is lowing through its teeth.

What do you call your father-in-law's only child's mother-in-law?
Mum.

What goes cloppity-clip?
A horse walking backwards.

What goes further the slower it goes.
Money.

Did you hear about the woman who bit her nails so much she took her stomach for a manicure?

Did you hear about the boy who slept with his head under the pillow?
The tooth fairy pulled out all his teeth.

What do you get when two strawberries meet?
A strawberry shake.

What do you get when two strawberries meet at a rock concert?
A strawberry crush.

What do you get when two strawberries meet at the waxing parlour?
A strawberry smoothie.

How many sides does a barrel have?
Two. Inside and outside.

Why do they call it a television set when you only get one?

Why are elephants grey?
So you don't mistake them for strawberries.

What has no legs or arms and runs downhill?
Rain.

What's the best way to stop food from going off?
Eat it.

How can you drop a raw egg onto a concrete floor without cracking it?
Concrete floors are very hard to crack.

How can you fill a page with writing using only two letters?
Write an SA.

If a butcher is six feet two inches tall, what does he weigh?
Meat.

What demands an answer, but asks no question?
A telephone.

What has knobs on the front and wobbles?
Jellyvision.

Why is nine drunk?
Because it's one over the eight.

What smells the most in a bakery?
Your nose.

Which animals can you eat before they are born and
after they're dead?
Chickens.

What is lower with a head than without one?
A pillow.

What is black when you buy it, red when you use it
and grey when you throw it away?
Coal.

Guess what I saw today.
Everything you looked at.

How can you stop milk turning sour?
Keep it in the cow.

What never asks any questions but gets lots of
answers?
A doorbell.

What's the definition of gorilla warfare?
Two monkeys fighting over a banana.

What is large, grey and has webbed feet?
An elephant wearing scuba gear.

What can you serve but never eat?
A volleyball.

What goes eighty miles an hour underground?
A mole on a motorbike.

What is a volcano?
A mountain with the hiccups.

How many telemarketers does it take to change a light bulb?
Only one. But he has to do it while you're eating dinner.

What grows when it eats, but dies when it drinks?
A fire.

Is it possible for someone to marry a widow's husband?
No, because the husband is dead.

When do you stop at green and go at red?
When you're eating a watermelon.

What is as sharp as a vampire's fang?
His other fang.

What's a prickly pear?
Two hedgehogs.

What goes into the water red and comes out black?
A red hot poker.

What's big, white, furry and always points North?
A polar bearing.

What is white and brown and eats hamster food?
A hamster.

What goes out black and comes back white?
A black dog in a blizzard.

Why did the doughnut go to the dentist?
It needed a chocolate filling.

When is a toilet angry?
When it has flipped its lid.

What dance can even the most wooden dancers do well?
The Balsa.

What food do you put in the refrigerator but it still stays hot?
Salsa.

What can a whole apple do that a half an apple can't?
It can look round.

If a gown is evening wear, what is a suit of armour?
Silverware.

What's the biggest rope in the world?
Europe.

What do you find at the end of everything?
The letter 'g'.

What's grey and furry on the inside and white on the outside?
A mouse sandwich.

What happened to the thief who stole a crate of prunes?
He's still on the run.

What do sailors say when they see a fat person on a ship?
'A vast behind.'

Which animal uses a nutcracker?
A toothless squirrel.

What has six legs, bites and speaks Norwegian?
A Norse-quito.

Why is a whale black and white?
Because if it was pink and white it would be a shrimp.

What is red, sweet and bites people in the neck?
A jampire.

Why do train drivers feel worried?
Because their job is always on the line.

Which has the higher IQ, latitude or longitude?
Longitude: it's got 360 degrees.

Why shouldn't you accept a cheque from a kangaroo?
It will probably bounce.

What word allows you to take away two letters and get one?
Stone.

If it took eight men ten hours to build a wall, how long would it take four men to build it?
No time at all: it's already built.

Why did the cowboy fire his gun in the air?
He wanted to shoot the breeze.

How can you spend hours on your homework every
night, and still get twelve hours' sleep?
Put your homework underneath your mattress.

Why is the letter 't' so important to a stick insect?
Without it it would be a sick insect.

Why are birthdays good for you?
Because people who have the most live the longest.

Why do you get a charge out of reading a
newspaper?
Because it's full of current events.

What's yellow, wiggly and dangerous?
A maggot with a bad attitude.

Why did the brain cell go to the other side of the brain?
I don't know. It hadn't really crossed my mind.

If a plane crashed on the border of England and Scotland, where would they bury the survivors?
You don't bury survivors.

Why did the man ask to be buried at sea?
So his wife couldn't dance on his grave.

How many animals did Moses take on the ark?
None, it was Noah.

What goes into the water pink and comes out blue?
A swimmer on a cold day.

Why do grape harvesters have noses?
So they have something to pick during the growing
season.

What is green and can jump a mile a minute?
A grasshopper with hiccups.

What's big and red and lies upside down in a gutter?
A dead bus.

Which three letters of the alphabet make
everything in the world move?
NRG.

What's red and looks like a bucket?
A red bucket.

Would you rather have a tiger eat you or a lion?
I'd rather have a tiger eat a lion.

When can you be three people at once?
When you are a mother, a sister and a daughter.

What kind of beans never grow in a garden?
Jelly beans.

When is a chair like a dress?
When it is satin.

What is round at each end and high in the middle?
Ohio.

Which two letters are always jealous?
NV.

Why did the gardener plant gold in the garden?
Because he wanted rich soil.

What has five fingers and drives a tractor?
A farm hand.

What does a dancer like to drink?
Tap water.

What kind of a degree do vets get?
A pedigree.

How many lighthouse-keepers does it take to change a light bulb?
Ten. Have you seen the size of their light bulbs?

What do you get when you have 324 raspberries trying to get through the same door?
A raspberry jam.

What didn't Adam and Eve have that everyone in the world has had?
Parents.

What did the girl say when the Statue of Liberty
sneezed?
'God bless America.'

What runs about all day and lies down at night with
its tongue hanging out?
A training shoe.

What's wet and wiggly and says 'how do you do'
sixteen times?
Two octopuses shaking hands.

What does a mineral swindler do to other minerals?
He gypsum.

What's the most dangerous part of a car?
The nut behind the wheel.

What did the shirt say to the trousers?
'Meet me at the clothesline. That's where I hang out.'

You're a bus driver. At the first stop four people get on; at the second stop six people get on; at the third stop three people get off; and at the fourth stop everyone gets off. What colour are the bus driver's eyes?
The same as yours because you're the bus driver.

What's taken before you can get it?
Your picture.

If there's a frog, dead in the centre of a lilypad which is right in the middle of the pond, which side would it jump to?
Neither, the frog is dead.

Romeo: I wouldn't marry you if you were the last person on earth.
Juliet: If I were, you wouldn't be here.

It's one hundred years old, but its head is only one night old. What is it?
Snow on a tree stump.

Why are there only eighteen letters left in the alphabet?
Because E.T. flew off in a U.F.O. and the C.I.A. chased after him.

What's yellow and flashes?
A banana with a loose connection.

Why is 2004 a good year for kangaroos?
It's a leap year.

What can you sit on, brush your teeth with, and eat soup with?
A chair, a toothbrush, and a spoon.

If a papa bull eats three bales of hay and a baby bull eats one bale, how much hay will a mama bull eat?
Nothing. There is no such thing as a mama bull.

What is a skeleton?
Bones with the people scraped off.

What looks just like half a loaf of bread?
The other half of a loaf of bread.

What did Rapunzel use to weave herself a rug?
An heirloom.

What has fifty legs but can't walk?
Half a centipede.

What has six legs and flies?
An airline pilot giving his cat a lift.

What's grey, has four legs and jumps up and down?
An elephant on a trampoline.

What has four legs, a tail, whiskers and cuts grass?
A lawn miaower.

What has forty legs and sings?
A school choir.

How many legs does a horse have?
Six: Forelegs in front and two behind.

In a swimming pool, four elephants were swimming.
Jamie jumps into the pool and from underneath
counts the number of legs. He counts only twelve.
How come?
One elephant was doing backstroke.

What has four legs and flies?
A picnic table.

What has eight legs and flies?
A dead donkey lying on a picnic table.

What happened when the chef found a daddy long legs in the salad?
It became a daddy short legs.

What has ten legs, no feet, no head, no arms and no hands?
Five pairs of trousers.

What has four legs in the morning and six legs at night?
A bed.

What's grey, has four legs and a trunk?
A mouse going on holiday.

What has four legs, is green and yellow, and if it
fell out of a tree would kill you?
Two bananas sitting on a pool table.

What has nine legs but can't walk?
Three stools.

What has three feet, but can't walk?
A yard stick.

What word only has three letters, but is longer
than dog?
Banana.

What has a bottom at its top?
Your leg.

What causes baldness?
Lack of hair.

What never gets any wetter, no matter how much it rains?
The sea.

In English what come after E?
N.

What happens after a dry spell?
It rains.

How do you spell 'hard water' only using three letters?
ICE.

What is the best way to get paint off a chair?
Sit on it before the paint's dry.

How many eggs does it take to screw in a light bulb?
None. Eggs don't have hands.

What kind of house weighs the least?
A lighthouse.

How many apples grow on a tree?
All of them.

If the red house is on the right side and if the blue house is on the left side, where's the white house?
Washington DC.

What goes 'Buzzzz, Zzzzub, Buzzzz, Zzzzub?
A bee stuck to a yo-yo.

What do antique clock collectors do when they get together?
Talk about the old times.

What's red and smells like blue paint?
Red paint.

You throw away the outside and cook the inside.
Then you eat the outside and throw away the inside.
What is it?
Corn on the cob.

Why did the clown wear loud socks?
So his feet wouldn't fall asleep.

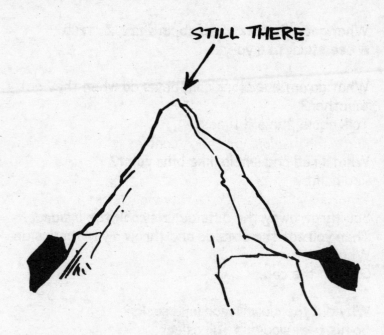

STILL THERE

Before Mount Everest was discovered, what was
the highest mountain on Earth?
Mount Everest.

What's a balanced diet?
A bag of chips in each hand.

What is a fibula?
A small lie.

Why did the clairvoyant cross the road?
To get to the other side.

What is black and white and white all over?
A scared skunk.

Where can you find cards on a ship?
On the deck.

What is always coming, but never arrives?
Tomorrow.

Can you light your birthday candles with two sticks?
Yes, if one of them is a match.

What do you get when twenty violinists start
playing at the same time but play different songs?
A senseless act of violins.

What goes up but doesn't come down?
A kangaroo stuck in a tree.

David's parents have four kids: North, South and East. What's the fourth one called?
David.

Who went into the tiger's den and came out alive?
The tiger.

What do you call a sad cow?
A blue moo.

Why is a room full of married people empty?
There isn't a single person in it.

How do you catch a school of fish?
With a bookworm.

When is a car not a car?
When it turns into a lay-by.

What kind of hat has fingerprints?
A felt one.

What is always behind time?
The back of a clock.

Why did the snail cross the road?
I don't know, he hasn't got there yet.

Why did the woman have pedestrian eyes?
They looked both ways before they crossed.

What's black and white, stinks and hangs from a line?
A drip dry skunk.

What's brown and yellow, brown and yellow, brown and yellow?
A monkey rolling down a hill holding a banana.

What floats on water as light as a feather, yet a thousand men can't lift it?
A bubble.

How deep is the water in a frog pond?
Kneedeep, kneedeep, kneedeep.

What kind of fish can't swim?
Dead ones.

What holds water yet is full of holes?
A sponge.

How many letters are in the alphabet?
There are eleven letters in 'The alphabet'.

When ducks fly in a V, why is one side of the V
longer than the other?
There are more ducks on that side.

What's black and white and makes a lot of noise?
A zebra with a starting pistol.

What's a mummy's favourite music?
Wrap.

What goes up a chimney down but won't go down a chimney up?
An umbrella.

What is white, tall and has ears?
A snow covered mountain.
But what about the ears?
Haven't you ever heard of mountaineers?

What do mummies put on their fingernails before going out?
Nile varnish.

How do you get fifty people to carve a statue?
Ask them all to chip in.

What can travel round the world while staying in a corner?
A postage stamp.

Why do hurricanes travel so fast?
Because if they travelled slowly, we'd have to call them slow-i-canes.

What did the sign to the cemetery say?
'Graveyard Dead Ahead'

What goes slam slam slam slam splosh?
A four-door spitoon.

What has three heads, is ugly and smells bad?
You. I was lying about the three heads.

What knocks you out each night but doesn't harm you?
Sleep.

Some months have 31 days. How many have 28?
All of them.

What did the skunk say to the other skunk?
'Say it, don't spray it.'

What goes over a bridge with water above and below but doesn't get wet?
A man with a bucket of water on his head.

Why is the sky so high?
So birds don't bump their heads.

What race always starts with a tie?
A three legged race.

What was Bob the Builder called after he retired?
Bob.

Why should you never tell a clock a secret?
Because time will tell.

If a rooster laid an egg on top of a barn, which way
would it roll?
Roosters don't lay eggs.

What did the cow say when it met the Queen?
'Moo.'

Did you hear about the pregnant snake?
She gave birth to a bouncing baby boa.

What kind of tree can you wear?
A fir.

What did one wall say to another wall?
'Meet you at the corner.'

What do clouds wear under their clothes?
Thunderware.

How can you say rabbit without using the letter R?
Bunny.

How can you tell if an elephant is sleeping in bed
with you?
He has a big 'E' on his pyjamas.

What can you put in a wooden box and still make it
lighter?
Holes.

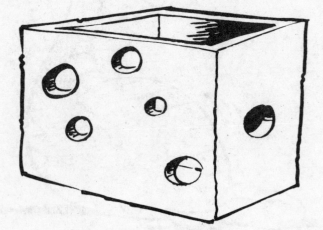

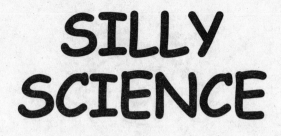

SILLY
SCIENCE

Mum to Dad: I think Jamie may grow up to be a space scientist. His teacher says he is taking up space.

Why doesn't anyone propose marriage to Saturn?
It has a ring already.

Last night as I lay in bed looking up at the stars, I thought to myself . . . where's the ceiling?

How do you find fish on the Internet?
With a perch engine.

What happened when the wheel was invented?
It caused a revolution.

What should you do if you get lots of e-mails saying,
'What's up, Doc? What's up, Doc?'
Check for Bugs in your system.

What is H2O4?
To drink.

What is copper nitrate?
Overtime pay for police officers.

Stuart: When I die I'm going to leave my brain to
science.
Jenny: I suppose every little bit helps.

When doesn't a telephone work underwater?
When it's wringing wet.

Jamie: This match won't light.
Sarah: That's funny – it did this morning.

What animal have you got inside your computer?
RAM.

How does fast light travel?
The same way slow light travels.

What happens if you get a gigabyte?
It megahertz.

Why do beavers spend a fortune on the Internet?
They never want to log off.

What is a baby computer's first word
Data.

Why don't you stamp e-mails?
Because your foot would go right through the
computer screen.

'Helpline? I've just pushed a piece of pork into my
disk drive.'
'Has the computer stopped working?'
'No, but there's a lot of crackling.'

I've got a good idea.
It must be beginners' luck.

Why is the law of gravity useful?
Because if you drop something, it's much easier to
get it off the floor than off the ceiling.

What is a chemical formula?
What chemists feed their babies.

Did you hear about when the two aerials got married?
The wedding was rubbish but the reception was great.

How do poor people send e-mail?
On the Skint-ernet.

Why did the germ cross the microscope?
To get to the other slide.

Why is the pen mightier than the sword?
Because no one has invented a ball point sword.

Stuart: If a person's brain stops working, does he die?
Jenny: You're alive, aren't you?

What did the big telephone say to the little telephone?
'You're too young to be engaged.'

Would you like to buy a second-hand computer?
I'm afraid not. I can only type with one hand.

What did scientists say when they found bones on the moon?
'The cow didn't make it.'

What is the centre of gravity?
The letter V.

What's a bird's favourite software?
Seedy ROM.

How did the skunk call home?
On his smell-ular phone.

Do you like web jokes?
Yes – they're e-larious.

What's a scientist's favourite pet?
A laboratory receiver.

How do you stop your laptop batteries from running out?
Hide their trainers.

SIMPLY
SHOPPING

What does an executioner do with a pen and paper?
Writes his chopping list.

Shoe shop assistant: How do your shoes feel?
Customer: They feel a bit tight.
Shoe shop assistant: Try pulling the tongue out.
Customer: Well, theyth sthill feelth a bith tighth.

Man: I would like to buy some stockings for my wife please.
Shop assistant: Sheer?
Man: No, she's at home.

Why do we buy clothes?
Because we can't get them for free.

Customer: I'd like to buy a mouse trap please, and hurry, I need to catch a train.
Shopkeeper: I'm sorry madam, but we don't have any that big.

Jenny: How much money have you got in your wallet?
Stuart: Between £140 and £150.
Jenny: That's a lot of cash.
Stuart: No, £10 isn't much.

Sign in shop window: 'Parachute for sale. No strings attached.'

What did the composer do before he went to the supermarket?
He wrote a Chopin Liszt.

Little Sophie stood in a department store near the escalator watching the moving handrail.
'Something wrong?' asked the security guard.
'No,' replied Sophie, 'I'm just waiting for my chewing gum to come back.'

How did the soldier pick up a new rucksack for five pence?
Because he always had an eye for a bergen.

Shop manager: I saw you arguing with a customer. Please remember that the customer is always right. What were you arguing about?
Sales assistant: He said that you're an idiot.

What do you get if you steal a calendar?
Twelve months.

Stuart: I've just bought a large pack of cards.
Jenny: Big deal.

Did you hear about the millionaire who had a bad accident?
He fell off his wallet.

Can I have a box of chocolates for my mum?
I'm sorry, we don't do swaps.

Did you hear about the stupid man who bought an AM radio?
He didn't want one for nights.

Why aren't my photos ready yet?
I'm sorry madam, I'm a late developer.

Whenever I'm down in the dumps I buy myself a new hat.
Oh, so that's where you get them.

Sarah: What was your mum's favourite subject at school?
Sophie: My dad says it must have been Buyology.

I got a CD player for my birthday with a one year guarantee. If it breaks down they guarantee it will be a year before they come and fix it.

What kind of underwear do identical twins buy?
Calvin Klones.

Why do bears buy cheap shoes?
Because when they wear them they still have bear feet.

What did the caveman buy his wife for Valentine's?
Nothing. He just gave her ugs and kisses.

When should you buy drainpipe trousers?
When you have water on the knee.

I hate shopping on the Internet, the trolley keeps
rolling off the top of the computer.

Where do dogs go when they've lost their tails?
A retailer.

Customer: Do you keep stationery?
Shopkeeper: No madam, I move around quite a lot.

489

Sign in shop: 'Guitar for sale, cheap, no strings attached.'

Shopper: How much are these tomatoes?
Grocer: Ninety pence a pound.
Shopper: That's expensive. Did you raise them yourself?
Grocer: Yes, I did. They were only eighty pence yesterday.

What do you call a person who can't stop buying carpets?
A rug addict.

Did you hear about the idiot who went shopping and was stranded for an hour when the escalator broke down?

WHACKO
WAITERS

How can you see flying saucers?
Trip up a waiter.

Waiter, waiter, what's the best thing that has ever
been served in this restaurant?
A writ.

Waiter, waiter, what can you suggest for a quick
snack?
Runner beans.

Bacon discovered the magnifying glass. At this
restaurant you need a magnifying glass to discover
the bacon.

Waiter, waiter, I can't eat this meat, it's crawling
with maggots.
Quick, run to the other end of the table and you
can catch it as it goes by.

Waiter, waiter, what's this I'm eating?
It looks like small chunks of chicken and large chunks of gravy.

Waiter: Would you like your coffee black?
Customer: What other colours do you have?

Waiter, waiter, I'd like to know what's in today's stew.
No, sir, you wouldn't.

Waiter: Sir, you haven't touched your custard.
Customer: No, I'm waiting for the fly to stop using it as a trampoline.

Waiter, waiter, do you serve breakfast at any time?
Yes, sir.
In that case I'll have bacon and eggs during the
Renaissance.

Waiter: How many pieces shall I cut your pizza into,
sir?
Customer: Oh, I couldn't eat more than six pieces.

Waiter, waiter, there's a small goat sitting on my
toast.
No sir, it's just a little butter.

Waiter, waiter, does the pianist play requests?
Yes, sir.
Then ask him to play tiddlywinks until I've finished
my meal.

Waiter, waiter, is the food here tasty?
Certainly sir. Eat here today and you'll still be able
to taste it next week.

Waiter, waiter, there's a mosquito in my soup.
Don't worry sir, mosquitoes have very small
appetites.

Did you hear about the restaurant that is so bad
that when they throw out the leftovers, the alley
cats throw it back?

Did you hear about the restaurant that is so bad
that the rats phone out for a pizza?

Customer: How much is a soft drink?
Waiter: Eighty pence.
Customer: How much is a refill?
Waiter: The first is free.
Customer: Well then, I'll have a refill.

How did the waiter get an electric shock?
He stepped on a bun and a currant went up his leg.

Did you hear about the restaurant that is so bad
that the customers say grace before, during and
after the meal?

Did you hear about the restaurant that is so bad
that the hot dogs are served with their tails
between their legs?

Did you hear about the restaurant that is so bad
that flies go there to lose weight?

Customer: This meat is too tough. I'd like the
manager.
Waiter: Sorry sir, he isn't on the menu.

Waiter, waiter, do you have a sheep's head?
No, ma'am, it's just the way I part my hair.

Waiter, waiter, I don't like cheese with holes.
Well just eat the cheese and leave the holes on the side of your plate.

What did the waiter say to the skunk?
'Sorry, I can't take your odour.'

Waiter, waiter, why is my apple pie all mashed up?
You did ask me to step on it, sir.

Waiter, waiter, I'll have the pie, please.
Anything with it, sir?
If it's anything like the last time, I'd better have a
hammer and chisel.

Waiter, waiter, I thought there was a choice for
lunch today.
There is.
No, there isn't. There's only cheese pie.
You can choose to eat it or leave it.

Waiter, waiter, take your thumb off my steak.
You want it to fall on the floor again?

Waiter, waiter, this fish doesn't taste as good as it
did last week.
That's odd, it's the same fish.

Waiter, waiter, what's this fly in my soup?
I don't know sir, I'm a waiter not a botanist.

Waiter, waiter, is there soup on the menu?
Yes, but I can clean it off if you like.

Waiter, waiter, send the chef here. I wish to
complain about this disgusting meal.
I afraid you'll have to wait, sir. He's just popped out
for his dinner.

Waiter, waiter, have you smoked salmon?
No, sir, I've only smoked a pipe.

499

Waiter, waiter, what do you call this?
Cottage pie, sir.
Well, I've just bitten on a piece of the door.

Waiter, waiter, have you got asparagus?
We don't serve sparrers and my name is not Gus.

Waiter, waiter, does the chef have pig's feet?
I can't tell, sir. He's got his shoes on.

Waiter, waiter, there's a twig in my soup.
Yes, sir, we've got branches everywhere.

Waiter, waiter, I'll have soup and fish.
I'd have the fish first if I were you, sir, it's just on
the turn.

Waiter, waiter, I'd like my steak well done.
Don't thank me, I haven't cooked it yet.

Waiter, waiter, there's a dead beetle in my soup.
Yes sir, they're not very good swimmers.

Waiter, waiter, why is my plate wet?
That's the soup, sir.

Waiter, waiter, there is a fly in my salad.
I'm sorry sir, I didn't know that you are vegetarian.

Waiter, waiter, I don't like the flies in here.
Well, come back tomorrow, we'll have new ones by
then.

Why do waiters prefer elephants to flies?
Have you ever heard anyone complaining of an
elephant in their soup?

Waiter, waiter, there's a spider in my soup. Send
for the manager.
It's no good, sir, he's frightened of them, too.

Waiter, waiter, is this all you've got to eat?
No, sir, I'll be having a nice shepherd's pie when I
get home.

Waiter, waiter, your thumb is in my soup.
Don't worry, sir, it's not that hot.

Waiter, waiter, bring me tea without milk.
We haven't any milk, sir. How about tea without
cream?

Waiter, waiter, this coffee is too weak.
Don't complain, sir. You may be old and weak
yourself some day.

Waiter: Tea or coffee, gentlemen?
First customer: I'll have tea.
Second customer: Me, too – and make sure the cup
is clean.
Waiter (later): Here are your two teas. Who asked
for the clean cup?

Waiter, waiter, there's a mosquito in my soup.
Yes sir, that's because we've run out of flies.

Waiter, waiter, there's a spider in my soup.
It's OK, sir, it's just catching the flies.

Waiter, waiter, this bread's got sand in it.
That's to stop the butter slipping off, sir.

Waiter, waiter, there's a fly in my soup.
Hold on sir, I'll get the fly spray.

Waiter, waiter, you're not fit to serve a pig.
I'm doing my best, sir.

Waiter, waiter, there's only one piece of meat on my plate.
Would you like me to cut it in two?

Waiter, waiter, will my pizza be long?
No, sir, it will be round like everyone else's.

Waiter, waiter, this soup is disappointing.
Why? What did you expect it to do?

Waiter, waiter, bring me a glass of milk and a Dover sole.
Fillet?
Yes, to the brim.